African Alternatives

Africa-Europe Group for Interdisciplinary Studies

VOLUME 2

African Alternatives

Edited by

Patrick Chabal
Ulf Engel
Leo de Haan

BRILL

LEIDEN • BOSTON
2007

This book is printed on acid-free paper.

ISSN 1574-6925
ISBN 978 90 04 16113 9

CONTENTS

INTRODUCTION

Patrick Chabal, Ulf Engel and Leo de Haan

Africa at the beginning of the 21st century

Africa is a remarkable continent with a large diversity of cultures, economies, political structures and landscapes—ranging from *kwaito* street life in South Africa to the nomadic Turkana way of life in Kenya, from the grinding poverty and hunger of the Sahel to the prosperous urban middle-class areas in Gaborone, from stable Senegal to state-less Somalia, from the (former) donor darling Museveni of Uganda to the (present) villainous Mugabe in Zimbabwe, from peaceful Ghana to war-torn Darfur, and from the scorching Sahara to the lush forests along the Congo river. However, in current representations of Africa two images stand out: poverty and violent conflict.

Poverty, first. The facts, indeed, are disturbing. Africa is home to 34 of the world's 48 poorest countries. More than 300 million Africans, out of 725 million, live in poverty, nearly twice as many as in 1981. And well over 40% of the world's population that lives below the poverty line is in Africa. The picture regarding economic growth is more positive with, for example, per capita GDP growth in some low-income countries reaching an estimated 3% for the second straight year in 2005. This is a marked improvement on the 1995–2004 Sub-Saharan African average annual growth of about 1.7%. However, it is too early to call this a trend and to relegate this first representation of Africa to the realm of fiction. Based on current estimates, most African countries will not meet any of the Millennium Development Goals (World Bank, 2006; Commission for Africa, 2004).

Violence, second. Here too the facts are far from cheerful. A large part of the world's conflicts are now concentrated in Africa. One in four African countries is currently suffering from the effects of armed conflict and around 20% of Africans are living in countries severely disrupted by conflict. Approximately 15 million Africans are internally displaced at present and another 4.5 million have sought refuge in neighbouring countries (ICG 2006). Nevertheless, the number of armed conflicts in Africa has recently declined. One of the longest running violent disputes—in southern Sudan—has come to an end. Sierra Leone has emerged from a decade of civil war and has taken up the challenge of reconstruction. Liberia too has become peaceful and now boasts the continent's first democratically elected woman president. On the other hand there is still very little progress in the deadly conflicts in Darfur and the Democratic Republic of Congo.

True as they may be, these two dominant contemporary representations of Africa, as a continent both poor and violent, have tended to distort our view of the ordinary African men and women who are successfully managing their lives—making a living and giving a meaning to what they do in an extraordinary demonstration of initiative and creativity, every bit as impressive as in other parts of the world.

This book aims first and foremost to stimulate the exploration of African initiative and creativity and thus to serve as an introduction to the themes taken up by the second AEGIS European Conference on African Studies, held in Leiden on 11–14 July 2007.

African Alternatives: Initiative and Creativity beyond
Current Constraints

There is no gainsaying that, at the beginning of the 21st century, Africa is facing a number of crises, such as failing states, war and poverty. Moreover, while China and India are rapidly increasing their share of world trade, Africa is lagging behind in the world economy. One question is how African countries can find a niche in an ever more competitive world market. Consequently, it might be thought that the analysts' task is to focus on the constraints that are restricting Africa's development and growth. However, we want here to centre attention on African agency and consider those new initiatives that are coming from African entrepreneurial activities, trade, self-help organizations, associational life, politics and religion at grassroots level.

Exploring such initiative and creativity is not limited to an understanding of the coping strategies of Africans faced with deteriorating socio-economic and political circumstances. Rather, the aim is to go beyond immediate conditions and analyze those initiatives that offer alternatives to the prevailing paradigms.

We hope to move away from the perspective of African 'victimhood' by stressing African 'agency', an approach now being adopted in many academic disciplines. Agency stands for manoeuvring space within and in interaction with a social, economic and political structure that is external to and, at the same time, part of agency itself. Agency is at the core of the creative process of social transformation but is mediated through the local actors' understanding, perceptions, ideas and needs. Whereas agency is limited by the opportunities available, African realities show time and again the (re)emergence of resilient configurations ranging from patterns of mobility, innovative forms of production to the creation of viable networks and associations. Any configuration is intimately linked to the economic, political and social position of an actor in society but, at a higher level, also with the analysis of power relations, the access to markets and resources, and the wider social relations in society.[1]

The first chapter in this book by de Bruijn, van Dijk and Gewald immediately sets the tone by presenting agency as an alternative to the view that the predicament of African societies is determined by structure. The authors first explore the origins of the agency perspective and then argue that African societies have always demonstrated the ability to negotiate whatever constraining ecological, economic and political circumstances they faced. Historically, the research focus on agency helped to put Africa back at centre stage after structuralist perspectives ended in an impasse. However, according to the authors, this research perspective requires much more than showing that Africans have agency. It demands painstaking empirical research that conceptualizes agency as simultaneously produced by actor and structure—that is a process of becoming rather than a state of being: agency as promise rather than premise. Interestingly, the authors caution development scientists and practitioners, who enthusiastically embraced the concept of agency in the last decade on the grounds that "it runs counter to the idea of makeability and, therefore, counter to interventionist paradigms that assume the possibility of guided if not 'mechanical' transformations of social realities...[whereas] agency [is] related to an unpredictability of outcomes of processes of change" (De Bruijn, van Dijk and Gewald: 15). According to the authors, there is no agency without reflexivity, which means that the study of African societies must not focus on customary

---

[1] Excerpt from the conference theme of the 2nd European Conference on African Studies (ECAS 2) Leiden 2007: *African Alternatives, Initiative and Creativity beyond Current Constraints.*

behaviour but on purposeful acting. And because histories in Africa are diverse, cultures vary just as much as expectations about the future: studying agency in Africa contributes to the general debate on social change.

Ricard's chapter develops an argument about African agency in the context of the literary contest between local and global. Arguing that the study of African literature must move beyond the easily accessible material written in one of the European languages, the author shows that attention to African-language literature opens up whole new areas of research and understanding. He gives evidence why, by giving priority to literature produced locally, an historically informed literary criticism can generate insights into the cultural framework that informs the lives and activities of Africans. At the same time, the study of such literature makes plain the myriad ways in which locally produced knowledge enhances agency in Africa. Ricard thus helps the reader understand that cultural agency is just as important to what is happening in Africa today as the more immediate vagaries of the daily strategies deployed by those who face difficult odds.

In her challenging review of issues of land rights and property Lentz demonstrates agency as purposeful acting rather than customary behaviour. In her historical yet topical analysis she unravels the discourses of autochthony, which are used to legitimize control over land and other resources. The question of what precisely is a first-comer group and who are the 'natives' and 'strangers' leads to a conceptualization of African land tenure as a flexible set of social relations to land, which adapt to changing political systems and economic constraints. Not only are today's land rights negotiable and politically embedded, but this was also the case with colonial and even pre-colonial configurations. So what was regarded as customary was in fact always purposeful. This insight helps to clarify not just the contemporary politics of belonging in African communities, but also illuminates current debates on the nation-state and citizenship.

As de Haan explains in the following chapter, the popularity of the 'sustainable livelihood approach' in development policy circles can in large part be explained by its focus on agency or "a pro-active self-help image [that contributes to]…improving the lives of the poor" (de Haan: 61). Contrary to top-down interventionist methods, this approach not only puts people's daily lives and needs at the centre, but also stresses their ability to escape from poverty and by doing so to achieve structural change. Although the chapter discusses the roots of the modern livelihood approach in current development policy debates, it concentrates attention on the analytical capacity of the approach to understanding poverty. The author shows how the livelihood approach, by putting more emphasis on the analysis of power relations, as is effectively done in gender studies, will enhance its sense of reality in Africa. This may also contribute to more contextualized ways of designing so-called pro-poor policies.

De Haan's plea to recognize that African livelihoods are increasingly becoming multi-local, links up very well with Bakewell and de Haas' chapter on African migrations. For its part, Frederiksen's chapter puts the spotlight on the livelihoods of African youth. There is of course widespread pessimism about African youth being a lost generation—captured by primitive politics, the violence of 'failed states' and global glorification of violence. However, she uses an actor perspective, common in livelihood studies, to examine their aspirations and survival strategies within the context of popular cultural practices. Her longitudinal study was a search for 'agency,' which she expected to detect in the popular culture of the youth's purposeful search for new informal economic opportunities. Her question is the extent to which the popular culture market contributes to political and economic empowerment, in terms of meaning and money. She concludes that young men indeed pursue new livelihood strategies such as migration, participation in politics and business opportunities by way of NGOs and religious institutions. Some succeed and others do not. However, they largely bypass the state and subscribe to the global institutions and agendas of world religions and universal human rights. There is thus no purposeful acting with respect to the state. As the youth only experience the state's control and coercive mechanisms, they do not acquire the knowledge and experience of democratic politics to press for reforms. The author finds this lack of self-confident engagement with local politics much more problematic than the influence of media or their engagement in popular culture.

Bakewell and de Haas wind up their chapter on African migrations with an interesting call for the study of the 'agency' of African migrants' processes of mobility. They suggest that the portrayal of African migrants as subjected to forces beyond their control is just a reflection of a more general representation of Africa as the plaything of powerful external forces. Modern discourses on African migration tend to represent it as an escape from poverty forced by violent conflict, environmental disasters or trafficking. The importance of social practices shaping migration from below is neglected. Most of their chapter is thus an attempt to dismantle the myths of African migration as being mainly Europe-oriented or concerned with the trafficking of women and children. They show that the bulk of African migration occurs within the continent and that there is no recent important increase in numbers. After examining the diversity of migration patterns in the continent's four macro-regions they conclude that there is much continuity between pre-colonial, colonial and post-colonial patterns, despite the significant impact of colonial rule. What strikes today is a diversification of intra-African migration patterns and a modest increase in migration out of Africa.

Interestingly, the following chapter by Cornelissen investigates the relationship between migration and the changing parameters of territory in Africa. Transit and settlement of migrants present challenges to the state because they constitute spaces separate from formal spheres of power. Migration is therefore considered as a form of reterritorialization that affects political authority and state sovereignty. After a review of how territory is perceived in analyses of political authority and statehood, the author focuses on South Africa and studies how distinct forms of migrant regimes affect power and sovereignty by looking at migration policy in the SADC context, the active production of physical and symbolic boundaries, and the informal routes and settlement of migrants beyond formal structures. The 'agency' of migrants results in purposeful action that stimulates the reframing of authority, in the sense that territorially defined statehood can no longer be maintained. Consequently, migration can be considered as a distinct process of reterritorialization, which changes the nature of power.

Van Beek's chapter takes off with a review of theories of tourism and a study of the characteristics of tourism in Africa. He calls for methodical relativism in the study of tourism in Africa, going beyond the 'good' and 'bad' dimensions, in order to come to grips with the various representations of Africa that tourists seek to experience. The chapter takes an interesting turn from the perspective of 'agency' when the author proposes an approach to tourism guided by the notion of the 'tourist bubble' as central to the dynamics of the tourist encounter. The bubble is the whole of the arrangements in which the tourists are encased, allowing them to view the outside whilst being protected from misfortune. It is therefore the bubble and not the tourist that interacts with an African guest society. Research into environmental factors, interest for the host community, study of host community related factors and of the contingencies of history would improve the understanding of the bubble. This would then make it easier to analyze the effect of the bubble on the host population.

> We also need to study initiatives and ventures in Africa that present alternatives to current discourses and encourage a theoretical debate on the representation of African voices and visions. An underlying question is how far African initiatives produce viable alternatives to current paradigms.[2]

The present collection of articles shows that African Studies offers a tremendous potential for comparison, which has hitherto only been partly exploited. Most papers build on intra-area comparison, except for Bakewell and de Haas. Others like de Haan, Cornelissen and van Beek try to test and evolve concepts for the African context, attempting at the same time, by adding contextual conditions, to refine causal claims. Van Beek's chapter may be considered to come close to a cross-area comparison. Finally, de Bruijn, van Dijk and Gewald go a long way towards redefining the concept of 'agency' for social science at large on the basis of their studies of 'agency' in various settings in Africa.

References

Commission for Africa 2004. *Our Common Interest. Report of the Commision for Africa.* London: Penguin Books (see also: http://www.commissionforafrica.org/english/report/introduction.html; accessed: 31 January 2007).

International Crisis Group 2006. *Annual Report* (see http://www.crisisgroup.org/home/index.cfm?id=4343&l=1; accessed: 31 January 2007).

World Bank 2006. *Millennium Development Goals.* Strengthening mutual accountability, aid, trade and governance (= Global monitoring report; 2006). Washington DC: The World Bank.

---

[2] Excerpt from the conference theme of the 2nd European Conference on African Studies (ECAS 2) Leiden 2007: *African Alternatives, Initiative and Creativity beyond Current Constraints.*

SOCIAL AND HISTORICAL TRAJECTORIES OF AGENCY IN AFRICA[1]

Mirjam de Bruijn, Rijk van Dijk and Jan-Bart Gewald

Introduction

Over the past four decades, all the major social-science paradigms from structuralism to Marxism, world-systems theory and globalization that sought to explain the predicament of African societies in terms of structure have been countered and critiqued by perspectives that emphasized human creativity and resilience, in other words 'agency'. One of the important contributions of the agency perspective to the academic understanding of social change in Africa has been its capacity to explode often victimizing approaches in exchange for a much more balanced understanding of the local processes at work in Africa. In this article this approach is taken as a challenge to a situation that developed around the year 2000 when African pessimism became a dominant perspective in much of the international development literature and in the media attention the continent received (see, for example, Anugwom 2004). The article develops an alternative interpretation of Africa's predicament by emphasizing the strengths of people, organizations and institutions in overcoming the constraining structures that are present in the everyday lives of many Africans today.

The promise of agency: Exploding the structure-actor dichotomy

Our discussions on the concept of agency and its relationship with social transformations were primarily informed by history and anthropology within African studies. In this debate, the essential dilemma for social and human scientists is how to grasp the dichotomy between actor and structure. Indeed, it is imperative that this dichotomy—

---

[1] This article is published in a longer version as introduction to the book (2007) 'Strength beyond Structure: Social and historical trajectories of Agency in Africa'. Leiden: Brill Publishers.

actor vs. structure—is addressed in an attempt to make sense of how people deal with their circumstances, however difficult perceptions of creativity, resilience and reflexivity in such conditions may be. For academia, this difficulty is related to the ways in which social science often presupposes a theory of structure in which the creation of dichotomies seems to be a necessary rhetoric and analytical tool. But it is also related to methodology. Our methodological 'tools' are probably not well enough developed to research the processes and dynamics that evolve in human societies in the negotiation between actors and structures. This article relies on empirical research and attempts to grasp what agency means in specific situations.

A view of African history indicates that, no matter how constraining circumstances can be in environmental, economic, political or social-cultural terms, African societies have demonstrated time and again numerous ways in which such conditions are negotiated in often unexpected ways. As Lonsdale (2000) has shown in his historical research, such conditions never become so totalizing or hegemonic that all creativity in countering or coping with the circumstances African societies are subjected to is annihilated. This specific approach to African history successfully negotiated the structuralist approaches of the 1970s and particularly influenced studies of resistance and rebellion in history by focusing on actors and agency. For example, Ranger (1999) and Youé and Stapleton (2001) emphasized the vision from within, highlighting the narratives of the people who lived through these transformations but in the process shaped them and gave them meaning. One cannot simply define a duality between changes from the outside and an actor's responses; on the contrary the inter-linkage and co-production between actors and these changes make for social transformations. To come to an understanding of these exceedingly complex dynamics, empirical realities need be at the centre of our analysis. In the historical studies the agency approach has put emphasis on the analysis of the complex dialectical interplay between actor and structure over time, indeed the emergence of agency in seemingly static and pre-determined conditions. There is a continual interplay, a truly dialectical relationship between social thought, as presented by historical actors, and the structure of the material conditions in which they live. It is in this complex interplay, in which neither is ultimately determinant, that agency emerges.

Parallel to this approach in the study of African history, we can situate the development of what has become known as the Manchester

School, linked to the Rhodes Livingstone Institute (RLI). Eventually, this School questioned early structuralism and structural functionalism in the study of Africa by turning its attention towards those kinds of social formations that countered or transformed elements of African life that in earlier studies had appeared as essential structures. The Manchester School opened up a perspective on the significance of institutional agency and the way in which African people appeared to produce networks and associations as formations in which this agency could be recognized, and which clearly transformed, for example, the structures of kinship. The debate around the concept of agency in the actor and structure dichotomy should also be situated in relation to the production of knowledge, in particular relations of power in our world. The RLI vision on the actor-structure relationship can be interpreted as a response to the colonial predicament of Africa in the 1950s and 1960s. In a sense, the actor-structure dichotomy was not only a product of analytical academic thought but also had a political role to play in a power-of-knowledge arena very much dominated by colonial and post-colonial practice, thought and rhetoric.

This birth of a perspective on agency became particularly relevant with the rise of Marxist interpretations of the African condition. The prevailing Marxist analysis of the underdevelopment of Africa in the 1980s was countered by actor-oriented models of development and modernization that emphasized the creation of so-called 'interfaces' as the meeting points where local societies would engage with the Western encroachment of capitalism. This transpired, for instance, in the work of Norman Long (1968, 1989), while Bierschenk *et al.* (2000) took the lead in the French discussions. Interestingly, feminist approaches have also been at the forefront of this discussion as the work of Henrietta Moore and Megan Vaughan (1994), amongst others, demonstrates. Furthermore, religious formations came to be seen as one of these interfaces, demonstrating the enormous symbolic creativity of African groups in mediating and negotiating this encroachment, also in immaterial terms (Comaroff and Comaroff 1993). In the mid-1990s, the Marxist tide definitively turned: social change came to be understood by looking at actors in terms of their decision-making, livelihoods and access to resources. This change was also visible in policy circles where democracy, decentralization and civil society became central in the discussion. Taking the dominant development of the underdevelopment perspective to task, the research focus on agency helped to put African people back at the centre of development policies (see, for instance, Kaag et al. 2004, de Haan and Zoomers 2005). The emphasis in these studies on agency has important consequences for the discussion about the development of Africa where it challenges the internationally recognized development models of the World Bank and other international institutions.

The rise of yet another leading paradigm in a structural understanding of the African predicament, namely that of world-systems theory and later globalization studies, appeared to produce a counter-discourse perspective on agency. Both paradigms would seem to provide a perspective in which Africa is perceived as a victim of processes that combine economic, political and cultural transformations on a global scale. This victimhood is often thereby described in two different trajectories that can be distinguished as 'push' and 'pull'. Firstly, in terms of push, globalization has meant that through such processes as SAPs (Structural Adjustment Programmes), Africa was pushed towards the market, to neo-liberalism, to specific ways of state formation, and to the acceptance of global structures and organizations. In terms of 'pull', globalization has resulted in the opening up of African societies to the global market, i.e. the enormous appeal of consumptivism, the introduction of ICT (Information and Communication Technologies), the media as well as the pull of international travel and migration, particularly to the West.

Other studies, as a reaction to this view of globalization, have demonstrated how a more balanced view of the manner in which African societies were affected by globalization should involve agency and the notion that a process of creative appropriation of globalization was well underway, as was evidenced by new social formations. In this approach, an attempt was made to bridge the actor-structure divide. Studies concentrated on new patterns of (transnational or transcultural) mobility, new religious bodies, conflicts over new resources and so forth (see van Binsbergen and van Dijk 2004, Clarke 2004, Nyamnjoh 2002, 2005). These insights have also led to debates on the relationship between society and the ecological environment, for instance, in studies on climate change (another form of globalization) where an attempt has been made to understand changes in the physical environment in relation to the actor's perceptions of his/her environment and vice versa (de Bruijn and van Dijk 2005).

These insights into agency research and analysis do not exist in a scientific vacuum. Sociologists such as Giddens (1987), Archer (2003),

Ortner (2006) and Emirbayer and Mische (1998) have formulated similar ideas about the relationship between structure and actor and introduced the term 'agency'. Also in studies on the relationship between the environment and society these ideas have been formulated by more theoretically oriented researchers. An important contribution in this respect was made by Ingold (2000) who emphasized the processual nature of the interaction between the natural environment, society and actors as processes of social change where transformations are situated in the dialectical linkages between actors and structure/context/environment, which he indicated with the term 'dwelling'. One cannot understand a structure without the role of actors and vice versa and it is this continuous dialectic engagement between actor and the environment that determines agency. Actors approach the structure and create it by their ways of dealing with their environment and, in doing so, influence their (physical) environment in such a way that it becomes influential to action and the actors themselves.

A similar example can be found in the ways in which global networks and structures have spread Pentecostal movements to African societies. At the same time, these local Pentecostal movements have produced transnational relations in the global domain. In so doing, the engagement with global structures of this particular religious ideology produces other new forms of global relations (van Dijk 2001, Gifford 2004).

If agency is simultaneously produced by actor and structure, it generates a reflexive and negotiating moment between the two. This is what we call a promise of agency, namely the teleological insight that both terms in the dichotomy are products of human action, intelligence, creativity, resilience and organization, and are therefore forever lodged in the making. Agency then is not perceived as a 'state of being' but as a 'process of becoming'. What was started by the RLI in studying agency, we propose, is still relevant in the context of the present-day juxtapositions to which individuals and communities are subjected on the African continent. If we take, for instance, Mamdani's dichotomized relationship between citizen and subject (Mamdani 1996) the promise of agency that should be put centre stage is the process by which both of these states-of-being are being negotiated by people, groups and institutes in a never-ending process of becoming. It is the promise of being not fully captured by either of the two states that feeds into an analysis of how people and societies produce the trajectories that move out of, mediate or negate these states of being.

Domains of creativity, inventiveness and reflexivity in this negotiation process are interesting fields to explore in relation to the realization of agency in the face of power hierarchies. Negotiations between individuals and their perceived (social and physical) environments and also between people are always informed by relations of power. Not only structures and actors act upon one another, but also the production of agency in various domains of society generates different power (im-)balances. In this process, new inequalities are produced and social hierarchies established. In our opinion this process is central to the forms of transformation that we observe in African societies.

Thus agency research should also explore the features of reflexivity and the way it becomes relevant in the economic, political, historical and socio-cultural domains of life of African individuals, groups and societies. By doing so we could move away from the naive view that people in Africa also 'have agency'. We instead emphasize how Africans realize agency, thus moving away from an ill-conceived premise of agency towards a promise of agency, i.e. reflections leading to agency that may or may not become fulfilled. The fact that we need to understand the social, economic and political conditions, constraints, opportunities for and ramifications of reflexivity as strengthening agency means that no easy assumptions can be made about what agency is or about whose hands it is vested in. This can only be demonstrated through detailed empirical research and can never be assumed or taken for granted.

Questioning processes of development

Though being the product of modernist thinking, these perceptions of agency and reflexivity stand in contrast to other modernist assumptions that emphasize or assume the makeability of society. These latter assumptions have not only had a long history in the social sciences in general, but particularly in the study of society in Africa. These included notions of society in which pre-conceived structural patterns of economic, political and socio-cultural life were extremely dominant. Structuralist traditions of social thought prefigured the existence of deep structures that would render the predictability of social behaviour possible. For instance, the envisioning of kinship structures in anthropology made predictable, or so it seemed, the ways in which marriage or inheritance relations are organized in African ethnicities. Likewise the patterning of economic relations, for example in terms of 'peasant' structures, domestic modes of production or livelihoods, seemingly attributes levels of predictability to the ways in which economic production, supply and demand, or even reciprocities appear to be organized. Without such structures predictability becomes impossible. Modernism in the social sciences thus provided the grounds on which projects of social engineering, such as in the form of 'development', could be envisioned on the African continent. It is in this respect remarkable that development theorists—as well as practitioners—have taken on board the concept of agency so forcefully as this runs counter to the idea of makeability and, therefore, counter to interventionist paradigms that assume the possibility of guided if not 'mechanical' transformations of social realities. If agency and reflexivity are related to an unpredictability of outcomes of processes of change that people, groups and societies initiate, the notion of 'development' becomes hard to conceive.

The premise of a structural patterning of social life has seemed to produce individual variation as a deviation from the general rule, a point well recognized and thus contested by the Manchester School. If, for example, a matrilineal system of inheritance predicted ego to inherit from his mother/brother, an inheritance from ego's father would likely be described as 'exceptional', as countervailing to the kinship system and thus anomalous. Yet from the individual's perspective, a reflection on and negotiation of what 'structure' would seem to predict may in fact be a sensible thing to do and be perfectly understandable in the context of prevailing circumstances or in the perception of an individual's understanding of things. In other words, the strength of a realization of agency should be recognized in the ways in which the individual would go about the constraints of such an inheritance system, thus calling for a better understanding of the kind of reflexivity that allows a person, group or institution to take a different course of action.

This problem of individual variation and of an inconclusive 'hegemony of structures' is not new to the modernist assumptions in the social sciences. However the research we conducted considers in particular how social situations appear to be governed by underlying or overarching principles and predicaments but still produce their own forms of reflexivity, their own forms of thinking about these structures and the actors involved that inform their agency.

Exploring the meaning of agency in Africa is to acknowledge the fact that the academic and the local interlocutor share in the production of structures and patterns as reflexive thought-constructs. Agency in other words is the on-the-ground refraction of the ways in which academics and locals alike perceive patterns, structures and predicaments that generate the contexts and frameworks in which action can be seen to take place. After all, the unpredictable only appears when looked at from the point of view of structure and pattern, hence from a position that is already abstracted from reality, something that exists at some distance from the lived realities on the ground and therefore has a reflexive dimension to it. Agency is about human capacity, i.e. this motivational strength to produce that reflexive distance, to monitor social behaviour from a reflexive distance, and to come up with opportunities and alternatives that are not 'automatic' but are inspired by the ways in which social realities always allow for many paths to be taken.

This search for how agency can be fruitfully studied on the African continent follows on from works such as those by Arens and Karp (1989), Jackson and Karp (1990), Honwana (1996), Ranger (1999), Comaroff and Comaroff (1993), Amselle (1998) and Lonsdale (2000), that have already hinted not at the uniqueness of agency but rather at the underlying strength of processes of reflexivity. While these studies may appear to have come close to a more or less western-informed philosophical reflection of African primordial modes of thought, they have not fallen into that trap. Instead, they have kept an open mind towards the specific African cultural, economic, social and political conditions that have shaped and transformed reflexivities over the course of time. Ethnographic questions such as who these thinkers are, who inspires action, in what terms this reflection is taking place, and what its constraints and opportunities are have all come to the fore. While Africanist research on agency has benefited from philosophical and sociological reflections on the concept, it has nevertheless created a specific ethnographic context for its understanding precisely because reflexivity cannot be taken or understood out of context.

Such a perspective on social realities in Africa is crucial to our understanding of current processes on the continent. Without being unduly optimistic about prevailing conditions in Africa in political, social or economic terms, the articles in this book share the notion that social behaviour is nevertheless not fully preconditioned by the structures these conditions appear to create. Social transformations *do* occur and their apparent unpredictability is often the result of an imperfect understanding of how people perceive and reflect on their condition, predicament and underlying structures. Following Ortner (2006) and Archer (2003), we posit that there is no agency without reflexivity; agency is not simply 'acting' but is reflexive, purposeful acting and directed towards a changing of the predicament, structure or condition that has been perceived in the first instance. Automatisms in acting or customary behaviour, such as shaking hands, can therefore not be considered as agency. Nor can 'actors' be perceived as 'having' agency as often so much of their acting is taken for granted and does not require or involve reflexivity of any kind. What people 'have' is their capacity and their strength to reflect on their situation, structures and actions in an attempt to look beyond their current constraints, however bleak their prospects for improvement may in fact be.

While many of the African societies deal with hardships of poverty, violence and uprootedness, reflexivity never dwindles; in fact reflexivity travels along the paths of coping, insecurity, destitution as well as along the paths of progress and prosperity. In each of these situations, 'actors' and 'structures' are matters of critical thought and reflection, subject to scrutiny and evaluation, and objects that in a sense are 'good to think with' that inform further steps. It is for this reason that agency prevents the local from being the victim of the global, the traditional being the slave of the modern, or the citizen being the subject of relentless authority. We think that the exploration of reflexivity directly links us to the creativity and inventiveness of actors, and that it is on this that research in agency should focus if it is understood as a process in the making, but also where actor and structure inform each other and in fact are one.

Conclusion

We have used the concept of agency so far as an analytical tool to explain social transformations in the societies the researchers have studied. Should we not also try to understand agency as an emic theory of causation as proposed by Gell (1998)? Ideas about agency are strongly related to the confrontations that people have in their lives. It is in confrontation that people come to define their own possibilities and agency. The strength of reflexivity apparently lies in its challenge and contestation.

Should we embark on the study of African agencies? Is there anything noteworthy about African agency? Perhaps not in essence, although differences clearly appear in the cultural way in which agency is expressed and is crucial for the social formations by which circumstances and conditions are negotiated, hence probably more in the context than in the people. Creativity and sociability are informed by culture and political relations. As such, the agency we find among Africans may differ from that among Europeans because histories are different, cultures vary and social relations are not the same, nor are expectations of the future. Here we enter the difficult debate on 'Africanity': is there something specifically African in agency as it develops on the African continent? We did not avoid this discussion, realizing that the risk in such a discussion is that it might essentialize what African is as it easily fits into victimizing Africa, thus creating a new exclusivism that does not further the discussion on social change.

In our view, the study of agency is doing justice to people's capability to reflect and act but is not losing sight of the structural circumstances that enable and constrain them. Agency is about the strength of people; but not unlimited. It is not sufficient to bring to the forefront the way people deal with long-term processes and structures: how they co-shape them should also be considered. Agency is about making a difference. This would seem to be clear but leads to a methodological problem of how to explore agency: how can we reflect upon somebody else's reflectivity?

Agency is a difficult concept to grasp in that it contains a lot of the values of the people who study it. Unravelling the concept of the agency of the researchers concerned should, therefore, always be part of a research project. In anthropology this is termed auto-ethnography. The researchers also have specific agency, creating space for reflexivity and intentionality while doing research. The way researchers do this is revealed in their texts and in the choices they make, for example, as to who to interview and who not, and which archives to read and which not. Increasingly Africans begin to reflect on the studies made of them, often leading to profound considerations of what academic literature has argued. By way of conclusion, it is remarkable to note that agency provides for a dialectical relationship between Africa and the researcher, much as it is forcing researchers themselves to become reflexive about their position in revealing Africa to others. Agency research not only reveals the psyche of the researcher but, more importantly, also the way this knowledge production has come about and how the researcher positioned him/herself in that regard. More than anything else, agency research has contributed to the strength of African studies in the present predicament of our understanding of Africa and of the ways academic reflections can and must be informed by African reflexivity.

References

Amselle, J.-L. 1998. *Mestizo Logics: Anthropology of Identity in Africa and Elsewhere*. Stanford CA: Stanford University Press.

Anugwom, E.F. 2004. *African Social Sciences and Development in the New Century: Challenges and Prospects*, African Development Review 16 (2) 399–414.

Archer, M.S. 2003. *Structure, Agency and the Internal Conversation*. Cambridge: Cambridge University Press.

Arens, W. and I. Karp (eds.) 1989. *Creativity of Power: Cosmology and Action in African Societies*. Washington DC: Smithsonian Institution Press.

Bierschenk, T., J.-P. Chauveau and J.-P. Olivier de Sardan (eds.) 2000. *Courtiers en Développement: Les Villages Africains en Quête de Projets*. Paris: Karthala.

Clarke, K.M. 2004. *Mapping Yoruba Networks: Power and Agency in the Making of Transnational Communities*. Durham NC: Duke University Press.

Comaroff, J. and J. Comaroff (eds.) 1993. *Modernity and its Malcontents: Ritual and Power in Postcolonial Africa*. Chicago IL: University of Chicago Press.

de Bruijn, M. and H. van Dijk 2005. *Introduction: Climate and Society in Central and South Mali*. In M. de Bruijn et al. (eds.) Sahelian Pathways, Climate Variability and Society in Central and Southern Mali. Leiden: African Studies Centre (= ASC Research Report; 78), 1–16.

de Haan, L.J. and A. Zoomers 2005. *Exploring the Frontier of Livelihood Research*, Development and Change 36 (1) 27–47.

Emirbayer, M. and A. Mische 1998. *What is Agency?*, American Journal of Sociology 103 (4) 962–1023.

Gell, A. 1998. *Art and Agency: An Anthropological Theory*. Oxford: Oxford University Press.

Giddens, A. 1987. *Social Theory and Modern Sociology*. Cambridge: Polity Press.

Gifford, P. 2004. *Ghana's New Christianity: Pentecostalism in a Globalising African Economy*. London: Hurst & Co.

Honwana, A.M.R. 1996. *Spiritual Agency and Self-renewal in Southern Mozambique*. London: School of Oriental and African Studies.

Ingold, T. 2000. *The Perception of the Environment, Essays on Livelihood, Dwelling and Sill*. London: Routledge.

Jackson, M. and I. Karp (eds.) 1990. *Personhood and Agency: The Experience of Self and Other in African Cultures.* Washington DC, Stockholm: Smithsonian Institution Press, Almqvist and Wiksell.

Kaag, M. et al. 2004. *Ways Forward in Livelihood Research.* In D. Kalb, W. Pantsers and H. Siebers (eds.) Globalization and Development: Themes and Concepts in Current Research. Dordrecht: Kluwer Academic Publishers, 49–74.

Long, N. 1968. *Social Change and the Individual: A Study of the Social and Religious Responses to Innovation in a Zambian Rural Community.* Manchester: Manchester University Press.

—— 1989. *Encounters at the Interface: Perspective on Social Discontinuities in Rural Development.* Wageningen: Pudoc.

Lonsdale, J.M. 2000. *Agency in Tight Corners: Narrative and Initiative in African History,* Journal of African Cultural Studies 13 (1) 5–16.

Mamdani, M. 1996. *Citizen and Subject, Contemporary Africa and the Legacy of Colonialism.* Princeton NJ: Princeton University Press.

Moore, H.L. and M. Vaughan 1994. *Cutting Down Trees: Gender, Nutrition and Agricultural Change in the Northern Province of Zambia 1890-1990.* London, Portsmouth, NH: James Currey, Heinemann.

Nyamnjoh, F.B. 2002. *'A Child is One Person's Only in the Womb': Domestication, Agency and Subjectivity in the Cameroonian Grassfields.* In R. Werbner (ed.) Postcolonial Subjectivities in Africa. London: Zed Books, 111–138.

—— 2005. *Images of Nyongo amongst Bamenda Grassfielders in Whiteman Kontri,* Citizenship Studies 9 (3) 241–269.

Ortner, S.B. 2006. *Anthropology and Social Theory: Culture, Power and the Acting Subject.* Durham NC: Duke University Press.

Ranger, T.O. 1999. *Voices from the Rocks: Nature, Culture and History in the Matapos Hills of Zimbabwe.* Bloomington IN: Indiana University Press.

van Binsbergen, W. and R. van Dijk (eds.) 2004. *Situating Globality: African Agency in the Appropriation of Global Culture.* Leiden: Brill Academic Publishers.

van Dijk, R. 2001. *Time and Transcultural Technologies of the Self in the Ghanaian Pentecostal Diaspora.* In A. Corten and R. Marshall-Fratani (eds.) Between Babel and Pentecost: Transnational Pentecostalism in Africa and Latin America. London: Hurst & Company, 216–234.

Youé, C.P. and T.J. Stapleton (eds.) 2001. *Agency and Action in Colonial Africa: Essays for John E. Flint.* Basingstoke: Palgrave.

ON THE POWERS AND LIMITS OF LITERATURE

Alain Ricard

In a recent special issue of *Research in African Literatures* (Fall 2006), Karin Barber and Graham Furniss call for renewed attention to African literature in indigenous languages. They notice that 'postcolonial literary theory has tended to overemphasize writing in English as the site of the postcolonial imaginary' (2006: 4). We could replace English by French and share the diagnosis! One of the effects of this over-emphasis has been 'a focus on the relation of postcolonial literature to the metropolitan centre and on the identity of the nation state.' It is time to read differently and to read different texts.

This is the kind of alternative approach on which we want to focus: writing in African languages compels us to redefine our conception of literature and provides a new context for understanding texts in European languages. We must rethink the articulation between local and global, and literary—verbal—practice is an excellent area for this kind of exercise. The weekly charts of literary magazines exist in what I call *mondoromanzo*, an analogy taken from the world of global winemaking: *mondovino*. In *mondoromanzo* the global bestseller overshadows all other kinds of verbal expression: fewer and fewer novels in French appear on these weekly charts, not to speak of novels in Dutch. Just as in *mondovino*, clever technician standardize wine production whatever the native soil, in *mondoromanzo* clever PR people produce 'above ground' literature, without any real roots.

Books are written in a language which is always a historical product. We non native English language speakers may write theory in English, but we write in our own languages when we write essays or poetry or fiction.

> Post colonial criticism was going even further than Commonwealth criticism in its effacement of modern indigenous language expression in colonized countries...replacing...a well meaning confusion with a definitive theoretical lock out (Barber 1995: 4).

Literary scholarship is on the wrong path if it emulates media and cultural studies which focus entirely on English medium productions: links cannot be cut to history, to time, to language and thus to philology. To achieve the alternative objectives needed for an African Renaissance, priorities must be set.

The first priority is the rewriting of literary history. The grand narrative of colonial imposition of European languages in Africa has to be contextualized, rewritten and long forgotten figures given due recognition. Literature provides us with many alternative memories that should be placed within the framework of this new history of literature. For instance, religious poetry such as the Nazarene hymns edited with a commentary by Gunner (2004) certainly belongs to this new history of literature! The second priority is the local literary scene and, of course, local languages. We need to edit, translate and comment on what is being done in these languages; we should remember that this material is difficult to grasp if we are not provided with historical information, which is too often lacking.

I will first give examples of what can be done, focusing on local literatures. At the same time I do not forget the world literary scene and the necessary African presence in that area. I conclude by proposing four pragmatic models of interaction between the local and the global scene offered to African authors.

Rewriting the history of literature

As we have remarked (Ricard and Veit-Wild 2005), African literature has long been used as a source of knowledge about life on the African continent, about colonial oppression, racism or gender. This legitimate interest is at the same time very reductionist. Writing from Africa should not merely be seen as a mirror of society. Scholars could question the status of literature within society and not only the image of the society within literary texts. Major writers have received far too little attention due to a lack of historical research and philological expertise. Karin Barber and Graham Furniss (2006: 14) insist on 'directing wide ranging questions to specific concrete texts or bodies of texts'. These questions fall into five categories: the interface with oral genres, the new written genres, such as the novel, the new ways of looking at the word, and, finally, new relations with the audience and an appropriation of literature for moral action (ibid.). This last theoretical stand is certainly not a novelty but in the *mondoromanzo* type of world novelistic economy it tends to be forgotten. A paradigmatic example of the Barber-Furniss approach is probably offered by the work of Thomas Mofolo, still widely read, but too often treated as if he were an Anglophone novelist. Africa is erased!

Thomas Mofolo (1877–1948) is best known as the author of *Chaka* (1926), a novel which today belongs to universal literature and has been translated into many languages. His first text, *Moeti oa Bochabela* (1907, French original translation: L'homme qui marchait vers le soleil levant, *The Man Who Walked Towards the Rising Sun*, 2003) makes him the first Sotho but probably also the first African novelist. This novel dominates Sotho literature and deserves more and special attention. A start is definitely provided by Kunene's excellent study (1989) which focuses on language. *Moeti oa Bochabela* is a prophetic and syncretic text, not a Calvinist demonstration, and certainly not an adaptation of the *Pilgrim's Progress*. Although it can possibly be read as a model of Sotho masculinity (Isabel Hofmeyer, *The Portable Bunyan*, 2004), the comparison with *Bunyan's* book, *The Pilgrim's Progress* (1954) does not help interpretation.

Fekisi, the hero, lives in the

> old times, when this land of Africa was still clothed in great darkness, dreadful darkness, in which all the works of darkness were done. It is the days when there was no strong chieftainship, the tribes still ate each other (Mofolo 2003: 37, my translation from the French).

Fekisi searches for God and, rejecting the customs of his Sotho ancestors, finds the light of the Orient on Mount Sion (2003: 153). On the Son of Man's invitation to follow him, Fekisi enters the holy city where he reigns with God because he had no fear and left his country for the love of God. To create a new genre, as Thomas Mofolo did, is not simply to tell a long story on paper but also to tell a story which incorporates what has made possible the very act of its writing. The novelist is acutely conscious of the creation of a literary language. He tells something that has never before been told: leaving his culture, starting towards a new horizon, crossing the sea, encountering new peoples. The narrative starts from within the culture, not from an abstract world but one permeated with the sounds and the words of Sotho villages.

There is an important moment in chapter five, in the middle of the novel, when Fekisi decides to leave his village. Instead of simply turning his back on the pagans as we tend to believe he did from superficial accounts of the novel compounded by bad translations, Fekisi returns to his *kraal*. He talks to his cows, as Chaka would do some years later in another novel. As we know, cows play a central role in the religion of the Basotho. Moshesh could not circumcize his son if he did not spread the offals of a cow on the grave of his grandfather. Cows are not merely a meat reserve; they are memory and religious artefacts. The French translation by Ellenberger makes this abundantly clear: 'la vache, intermédiaire divin' in notes as well as in precise translations of Sotho terms. Where in English we have the 'girls', Ellenberger in French translates the Sotho term as the 'initiates', thus, telling quite a different story!

So what is our 'proto' Christian doing with these sacred cows? Are they not a hindrance to his progress as a Christian? What emerges from this chapter, a central chapter in the book, is not exactly the picture of a devout Christian rejecting his entire culture. Fekisi dreams, praises and then leaves. This is the individual quest of a man who is totally immersed in his own culture and who does not condemn the initiates, the *bale*. On the contrary, the animals are almost accomplices, encouraging him to go. This scene is extremely important. By performing the praise song, Fekisi places himself squarely within his culture and it is surely not a detail if he does so at the time of his departure. What is new in the novel is precisely this syncretism: verbal syncretism of praise eulogies spread throughout the narrative, as Kunene convincingly shows, and religious syncretism as we have tried to show. In a world heading towards separate development, this practical apologia of syncretism was doomed to fail and to remain misunderstood. In any case its subversive content was erased.

If the figure of the writer is partly the figure of a prophet, then Mofolo could be considered one of the Bantu prophets. As Paul Ricoeur (1983) would express it, the novelist reconfigures the world, gives a new figure to feelings and representations. He also creates a new language, still waiting to be used again. This is what the oral poet does with tradition. *Moeti oa Bochabela* reconfigures, in Paul Ricoeur's sense, the world experience of a Sotho shepherd in a totally new way. It is the story of a conversion, of a solitary adventure, in a society viewed by an individual who presents in a new way what has always been there.

Another example of an important and neglected figure is David Yali Manisi, an oral poet, an *imbongi*, reknown in the Thembu area, but unknown outside. Jeff Opland met him in 1970 and started a fruitful association with him up until the mid nineties. David Yali Manisi had celebrated the famous Thembu chiefs and their associates. In the fifties he had composed poems to celebrate Kaiser Mathanzima, Sabatha Dalindyebo, and Nelson Mandela. Some of his poems were published in book form by Lovedale Press but remained unknown. Poetry in Xhosa was considered long dead: who was interested in such linguistic practices? Who mentioned them in the histories of literature in Southern Africa? Jeff Opland had studied medieval poetry; he was aware of the debate surrounding the oral nature of Homeric poetry and he realized that what Manisi was doing was exactly what Homeric scholars had studied in the Balkans a few decades earlier. He started to record and to translate Manisi's poems; he also edited them. In 1983 he published a groundbreaking book, *Xhosa Oral Poetry*, then in 1998 *Xhosa Poets and Poetry*, and finally in 2005, *The Dassie and the Hunter*, a personal account and analysis of his long association with the poet in the context of apartheid South Africa. A member of the African National Congress in the 1950s, David Yali Manisi was the official poet of the Transkei in the 1970s, one of the earliest Bantustans. His poems are impressive, even in translation: long, vibrant, full of images, direct. We can see clearly the filiation between his oral and literary style and rap poetry.

> Unlike the poetry of Mqhayi, Manisi's poetry is neither well known nor widely appreciated. It needs to be understood as the product of one exponent of a well established tradition, a tradition in the process even now of redefining itself...(Opland 2005: 26).

This quote from Opland shows the extent of rewriting of history in which we need to connect contemporary 'bush' poets with well known literary figures: the tradition is not only the Xhosa tradition, it is the tradition of Oral poetry, and of its philological study. But to be able to know and appreciate these texts you need to undertake field research: philologists seldom do that these days! Few scholars with a background in general and comparative literature have studied African literature. What Opland has accomplished is truly remarkable because it maps for us a new province of African literature.

Examples of creativity and originality can be found in other linguistic areas. Mulokozi and Sengo's work on *History of Kiswahili Poetry* (1995) is a good example of the mapping of a new terrain. Mulokozi has studied the works of Habibu Selemani, a Muhaya poet and master of Enanga poetry in his book, *The African Epic Controversy* (2002). The impulse behind these seemingly diverse projects is the same: the need to rewrite the history of literature in Africa, the need to foreground

original creative artists, too often neglected because of scholarly linguistic incompetence: again fieldwork is needed, not very rewarding
at first and time consuming. Literary scholarship is also a branch of
linguistic anthropology.

At the same time ideological factors were at work: the new intellectual elites who have mastered European languages claim a monopoly
of discourse and a unique understanding of tradition. They project
a rupture between oral and written literature which is absent in
David Yali Manisi. This is not in line with older, native, indigenous
modes of discourses, which for instance claim an African appropriation of Christianity or of Islam. Words and concepts from the native
languages—*morena*: king in Sesotho for instance—are reinterpreted.
The philological commentary is an hermeneutic exercise. The work
of Elizabeth Gunner on Shembeian hymns is also truly groundbreaking in that sense in showing the combination of Zulu poems and
Christian hymns. But the new forms bring new messages: Shembe's
histories promote a rejection of the 'macho heroic ethic of warrior
leadership' (Gunner 2004: 40) which has been the cornerstone of
Zulu traditionalism from Chaka to Jacob Zuma! These hymns are a
beautiful collection of African poetry in Zulu, but they were the sole
patrimony of an African church until Elizabeth Gunner edited them
with a commentary. Her work allows us new insight into Mofolo's
prophetic wanderings in Southern Africa by inviting comparison with
the narrative testimony of Meshack Hadebe (in Gunner 2004), one of
the first writers from the Nazareth church.

The examples given above are typical of the rewriting being undertaken by some scholars of the history of literature in Africa. An African
Renaissance, a true set of alternatives, requires these efforts. There
will not be an original African literature if the work of African language pioneers and practitioners is not understood, studied, taught.
This does not mean that there is a 'true' African literature only in
African languages, just that important areas of African expression
have been erased or neglected and that they should be brought to
our attention.

Local languages

What Mofolo had to say needed a new language: in his case it was
prose fiction, which he invented as an artistic medium in Sesotho.

The situation is the same in many languages if we assume from the start that the choice of language is the choice of a social and linguistic method in constructing an artistic world. This spiritual experience is thus a political gesture of a very practical kind, unfortunately tainted in many cases by the suspicion of an inferiority complex. Did these authors write in Shona or in Yoruba, because they could not write as successfully in English? Did others write in Kiswahili in the nineteenth century because Arabic was too difficult? This suspicion is very powerful and very harmful: it negates the positive component of language choice in favour of an instrumental strategy, of a so-called worldly wisdom that smacks of condescension. We can, with some imagination, understand the aspirations of these writers and respect their efforts. For several years I studied people who wrote in a minority language and felt that it was terribly wrong to reduce their choice to one by 'default'. These writers were often defenders of Christian (Kitereza 1980, Mnyampala 1965) or Muslim (Robert 1991) 'middle class' values, which had little appeal to cosmopolitan nationalist intellectuals or committed scholars. Some of these writers were mid level civil servants, or even catechists, had a family and children, did not have much money and seldom travelled: nothing fancy! They did not belong to our stereotype of the 'poète maudit', they were not a 'lost generation': they even tried to be models for their own people! Yet the political and ethical questions they posed—in the area of education for instance, on the meaning of tradition—were at the centre of efforts to produce a written version of their language in today's world. Should dialects be given a place? Should the standard language be chosen? What is the ethical value of traditional poetry if it promotes only values of violence and hierarchy? If, like in Rwandese 'Poèmes dynastiques', it is full of bloody killings? (Ricard 2005: 250).

At the same time, one never writes what one speaks: the creation of a written language is a dialogic process. What is written is an historical product handed down by committees, refined after countless hours of discussion, the product of a negotiated consensus. Can literature accommodate this spirit of consensus? When Serb and Croat diverge and there is no longer a Serbo-Croatian language, we see the linguistic harm done by the absence of a spirit of consensus. The writer is torn between a necessary language consensus and his own idiosyncratic view of the language and the world. Literature is first a practice, an 'artisanal' practice, and not a series of reified artefacts: it is a process, and not a product!

Very few complete studies treat African writers as historical subjects trying to find a personal voice. The biographies of Dhlomo and Plaatje (1930), for instance, are all too rare examples. It is as if the stigma of elitism was attached to literature. Writers were too often felt to be aspiring petty bourgeois, if not real bourgeois; after all, Mofolo became a successful mine recruiter… Writers did not have the romantic appeal of the native perfomer for the anthropologist or of the peasant masses for the sociologist. I talked to many writers and was struck by their lucidity. In a way they are, by their very work, protesting against the uniformization of the world, against the domination of so-called world or imperial languages, be they English, French or Mandarin Chinese. The very act of writing one's own language in a creative way is an act of resistance against the posturing of globalization, the fallacy of monolingual multiculturalism. Africa has to be treated like the rest of the world and we have to translate and edit African texts to encourage young aspiring writers. Publishing at first abroad is not the only way to be read globally. Local relevance, philological expertise, verbal mastery have their own convincing 'global' dynamics! Our optimistic view is that a successful local writer will eventually achieve exposure to a broader world audience.

Local literatures, global audiences?

It has long been my conviction that the discussion and study of African language literatures is a major alternative to the reductionism of the so-called multiculturalist approach to literature. Multiculturalism without multilingualism is mere—well meaning?—posturing! But very few non native speakers are able to read works written in African languages. This narrow readership, narrow in the sense of shared cultural assumptions, is empoverishing African literatures. It took me, for instance, seven years to publish a translation prepared by former students of mine of *Amegbetoa*, a standard Ewe novel, unknown outside Ewe culture. *Amegbetoa* exists now in French. When I put it on the reading list of my African literature course, two years in a row, along with *Chaka*, I was extremely surprised by the positive reaction of young French students. They were fascinated by the story of a young man in search of justice, of the suffering of a just soul in pre-colonial Africa, in an Africa marked by its own social dynamic, and also its wars. *Amegbetoa* has a universal appeal, a sad austere quality that we find sometimes in Ewe singing. This beauty was felt by the students.

This was also the case with *Chaka*, an extraordinarily ambiguous book marked by a plurality of voice, where the Sotho tradition and heritage of negotiation is contrasted with the Zulu war tradition. In praise poetry and epic song one voice is heard. In *Chaka* the small voice of individual conscience is heard as well as the powerful voice of the group set against the examples of several possible ways to deal with the future. Why did such a powerful writer stop writing? In his excellent book, *Thomas Mofolo and the Emergence of Written Sesotho Prose* (1989), Dan Kunene provides a context of understanding through a careful philological reading but no definite answer. From my own study of Hussein (Ricard 2000) and risking a parallel, I would say that poor translations, resulting in simplified works with complexities and contradictions purposely (?) left out, may explain his silence.

My interest has long been for small regional languages, but whereas Dutch, Danish and Greek, for instance, have fewer speakers than many African languages, they are not considered inferior languages. African languages have been marked by a history of racism and denial of the capacity for intellectual achievement. For obvious reasons it is usually very difficult to make a comparative assessment of the literary situations in Zulu and in Yoruba, or in Kiswahili and in Hausa, or Amharic. Throughout the last three decades I have met with many African language writers. I have talked to them about their reasons for choosing to write in an African language, about their hopes, their frustrations. I also tried to publish works in translation with limited success. I adhere totally to what Edouard Glissant (1981: 318), the West Indian poet and thinker, said a quarter of century ago: that languages not written in the next century run the risk of slowly dying and that their situation is probably the symptom of a deeper spiritual and intellectual crisis.

In many African language literatures, creative writing is in a special predicament. It has a captive readership composed of school children and is often written by authors enjoying the sanctuary and prestige of language boards. This is economically satisfying for a few specialized publishers but is not the usual situation in which literature develops. Criticism is too often limited to language teachers and emphasizes educational problems. Few readers from outside the language community propose an interpretation; translations from other literatures are limited to excerpts from classical works. A modernist and innovative writer runs the risk of being neglected and not understood. But if recognition does not come from the linguistic community—the group of speakers and readers of the language—it will not come from without since so few works are translated. They may even be asked to translate themselves, a kind of spiritual *harakiri* for some of them, who refuse to obey the dictates of the captains of *mondoromanzo*! This is often the predicament of the writer in an African language. Most are bilingual but are not translated...Some African languages have a century old written literature, but in many cases these literatures are in intensive care. The example of Ebrahim Hussein, once the most famous playwright in Kiswahili, who has voluntarily stopped to write, is perhaps an indication of a predicament that may affect other writers. I believe that it is in the area of translation that a special effort has to be made to encourage writers and to let wider audiences share the experiences and the meanings offered by these works.

In Zimbabwe, writers like Charles Mungoshi and Chenjerai Hove chose to write and publish in both English and Shona. Their example in the seventies probably encouraged James Ngugi to break away from the format of the English modernist political novel and to create in his own language, Gikuyu, the first real novel (a long prose text and not a pamphlet). Pugliese (2006) discusses this question in a fascinating paper, providing historical depth to our reading of Ngugi. Ngugi articulated the theoretical basis of his break with English in several essays, especially *Decolonising the Mind* (1986): for him the only true 'African' literature is in an African language. His influence has been felt in a similar posture (break with the Europhone tradition) taken recently—and momentarily?—by Boris Boubacar Diop, for instance. We should, however, remain focused on those writers who have kept publishing in their own language and did not feel the need to publicize a long delayed, and sometimes short-lived, conversion. The novels of Mohammed Said Mohammed, Euphrase Kezilahabi, Said Ahmed Mohammed, W. Mkufya (see Garnier 2006) are already an important body of writing, which needs to circulate in translation and which shows what it means to write in one's own language.

It is thus very important to discuss Ngugi's break with English as a political posture and to place it against the backdrop of a continuous practice of writing in Kiswahili. The fact that these Tanzanian works have not been translated into English is just a testimony of the refusal to acknowledge cultural biodiversity: how can we expect to bridge the digital divide if we are not even capable of bridging a literary divide.

Not a single modern Swahili novel (after Shaaban) has been translated into English! This is a kind of cold war waged against cultural diversity: no attention is paid to what is being said in Kiswahili; the only Tanzanian writers worthy of western media attention are long time expatriates in Toronto or London, who seem to capitalize on the appeal of Orientalism which is very successful in the West and in the North, and to benefit from the lack of translations of their Tanzanian colleagues. The same is true of an excellent—but mysterious—book like *Abyssinian Chronicle*, of which the original text (*Abessijnse Kronieken* (1998)) seems to have only a virtual reality: should we retranslate it from Dutch into English? Where is the manuscript: is it in English, in Dutch? Traceability is also required for this new brand of global cultural product!

Towards a typology?

From what I have written so far it is clear that I give high priority to local initiative, to what is expressed about Africa, from inside Africa, whatever the place or the language—African or European. Collecting more than eighteen hundred (1800!) pamphlets and novels in Hausa over the last decade, as Graham Furniss did, is testimony of the vitality of indigenous enterprise and publishing. Scholarship is too often written from outside, without contact with the sites of cultural production. The creation in the University of Kwazulu Natal of a *Centre for African Literary Studies*, the celebration in Dar es Salaam of the 75th anniversary of TUKI, the commitment by a South African Foundation to salvage and publish Timbuktu manuscripts are efforts going in the direction of reclaiming African scholarship for Africa. The continent's politics put a heavy burden on any practicing intellectual. He has to negotiate his position in his own society—the writer needs a language community; but he also has to have means of survival and, thus, an audience and the more global the better. I would like to propose a typology of attitudes chosen to deal with these constraints and to distinguish between embedded, diasporic, nomadic and commuting writers.

To be active in whatever language, on the local scene, is to be embedded: to have a local audience, in English, in French or in an African language. This is a new kind of commitment, perhaps the only commitment which is possible in today's Africa! Of course, within the local production African language books can be found. Femi Osofisan, the Nigerian poet and playwright, lecturer and journalist is a model of the embedded writer. Literature produced and read in Africa and quite obviously African language literature is our first, but not exclusive, concern. Too little is written on such literature for lack of information. However, distribution networks for African published books are starting to be developed (*Afrilivres, African Book Collective*) and bring to the North books published in the South. Journals can now be consulted on the net: *Kwani* in Kenya, edited by Binyawanga Vainana, *Litnet* in South Africa (http://www.litnet.co.za).

In former Zaire, in the 1970s and the 1980s, the great name of local literature was that of Zamenga Batukezanga, a novelist and philanthropist. He became the founder of an association to help the handicapped and was greatly respected for his social work. His books—narratives, novels—became well known inside his country but largely unknown outside. He was a perfect example of the writer practicing his craft to generate moral action, and he was doing it in French, verifying the remark that the language distinction is less salient in such works (Barber and Furniss 2006: 13) and that what is important is the local readership. Zamenga's generous outlook, his moral sense, his narrative abilities, made him the representative of a kind of commitment too often overlooked from abroad: a writer deeply embedded in his own society. Literature is truly for him equipment for living a better life, for reflecting upon values, for promoting solidarity and human respect. This kind of writer may seem very far from the dominant model in the North, but is a true alternative writer! Who could say that literature as a human enterprise is not well served by that bias?

Too often young writers are ignorant of the history of their people's literature: as we tried to show with Mofolo's example, much remains to be done to make it available to younger generations. It is easier to find any English Lit primer than to discover erudite editions of Swahili tenzi or Zulu praise poems. Fortunately some younger writers know their language history and have some sense of a literary heritage: for example, Nhanhla Maake, C.T. Msimang and M. Mulokozi. They belong to the category that I call embedded writers. Like many Tanzanians writers, working in Kiswahili, they live and work in their country and do not feel a need to write in another language.

The opposite attitude is that of writers who are considered by others to be African writers but who are perhaps more representative of a so-called diasporic imaginary community: Tanzanian writers in exile, writing in English, Francophone Africans who have lived for a very long time in Europe, refugee writers who thematize their predicament but are somewhat detached from Africa and sometimes proud to be that way. The question of traceability then becomes important because diaspora is a real market, which tends to capture for their sole benefit the Northern and Western readership. Issues generated by the world success of *Abessijnse Kronieken*, come easily to mind. Diasporic books rarely make it to Africa. Their authors are successful expatriates and I do not think they can have much impact on their literary language community.

More interesting categories would be the nomadic and the commuting writers. The examples of the great commuter Wole Soyinka and of the emblematic nomad, Nuruddin Farah, come to mind. Wole Soyinka keeps his home base in Nigeria: he runs projects, has created a Foundation, commutes between Nigeria and the North where he can raise money and if need be, seek refuge. I believe he offers a convincing alternative of what an African writer's career can be. I think he has some influence on younger writers who understand that freedom can be gained at such a cost: many younger writers practice Soyinka's kind of dynamic and productive commuting, for instance Kangni Alem (2002).

Nuruddin Farah's attitude is different but presents the same commitment to Africa, even if his country is no longer on the map. Farah will not go into exile outside of Africa. He could become an expatriate, leaving the African continent, but refuses to do so. He has lived and taught in Nigeria, Uganda, and now South Africa. He is still a Somalian, but there is no Somalia. In one of his last books (2000) he travelled to meet with refugees from his country. He presents a nuanced picture of individual trajectories. In his novels he has analyzed the system of dictatorship. What is important is not the language he writes in, but the commitment he keeps to the welfare of Africa, to a solidarity with the continent, to a community of destiny. This is what makes Farah, like Soyinka, an African writer. If need be, or if possible—and it is not possible in Somalia—they remain embedded and do not aspire to perform solely on the diasporic scene. They are too well aware of the *mondoromanzo* type of posturing. Africanist scholars should also be aware of such confusion and take time to trace works, to contextualize and historicize them, as Opland, Gunner and Mulokozi do. The only alternative to the virtual Africa of *mondoromanzo* is the Africa that speaks, screams, writes: the Africa that produces ideas and verbal forms, the literature of Africa.

References

Alem, K. 2002. *L'Atterrissage, suivi de: Dis moi, à quoi ça sert un écrivain en Afrique?* de Emmanuel Dongala. Libreville, Ndzé.
Batukezanga, Z. 1982. *Souvenirs du village.* Kinshasa: Ed Saint-Paul Afrique.
Barber, K. 1995. *African language literature and Post colonial Criticism*, Research in African Literatures 26 (4) 3–30.
Barber, K. and G. Furniss (eds.) 2006. *Special Issue, Creative Writing in African Languages*, African language writing, Research in African Literatures 37 (3) 1–14.
Bunyan, J. 1954 (1678). *The Pilgrim's Progress.* London: Dent.
Couzens, T. 1985. *The New African, A Study of the Life and Works of H.I.E. Dhlomo.* Johannesburg: Ravan Press.
Farah, N. 2000. *Yesterday, Tomorrow, Voice from the Somali Diaspora.* London, New York: Cassel.
Garnier, X. 2006. *Le roman swahili.* Paris: Karthala.
Gérard, A. 1971. *Four African Literatures: Xhosa, Sotho, Zulu, Amharic.* Berkeley, Los Angeles CA: University of California Press.
—— 1984. *Thomas Mofolo ou les oublis de la mémoire française*, Politique africaine 13, 8–20.
Glissant, E. 1981. *Le Discours antillais.* Paris: Le Seuil.
Gunner, E. (ed./translater) 2004. *The Man of Heaven and the Beautiful Ones of God*, Umuntu waseZulwini nabantu abahle bakaNkulunkulu. Scottsville: University of KwaZulu Natal Press.
Hofmeyr, I. 2004. *The portable Bunyan.* Johannesburg: Witwatersrand University Press.
Isegawa, M. 1998. *Abessijnse Kronieken.* Amsterdam: De Bezige Bij.
Kiteresa, A. 1980. *Bwana Myombekere na Bibi Bugonoka na Ntulanalwa na Buliwahli.* Dar es Salaam: Publishing House.
Kunene, D. 1989. *Thomas Mofolo and the Emergence of Written Sesotho Prose.* Johannesburg: Ravan Press.
Mnyampala, M. 1965. *Diwani ya Mnyampala. Amsha*, Dar es Salaam: Eastern Africa Publications.
Mofolo, T. 2003 (1907). *Moeti oa Bochabela.* Morija: Morija Sesuto Book Depot, 1907. (French original translation, L'homme qui marchait vers le soleil levant, translated by V. Ellenberger. Bordeaux: Confluences).
—— 1910. *Pitseng.* Morija: Morija Sesuto Book Depot.
—— 1981 (1926). *Chaka.* Morija: Morija Sesuto Book Depot, 1925 (English translation: Chaka, a New Translation, by D. Kunene, London: Heinemann).
Mulokozi, M. 2002. *The African Epic Controversy: Historical, Philosophical and Aesthetic Perspectives on Epic Poetry and Performance.* Dar es Salaam: Mkuki na Nyota.
Mulokozi, M. and T.S.Y. Sengo 1995. *History of Kiswahili Poetry.* Dar es Salaam: TUKI.
Ngugi Wa Thiong'o 1986. *Decolonising the mind.* Oxford: James Currey.
Njogu, K. 2004. *Reading Poetry as Dialogue.* Nairobi: The Jomo Kenyatta Foundation.
Obianim, S. 1990 (1949). *Amegbetoa, alo Agbezuge fe nutinya.* London: Macmillan (French original translation, Amegbetoa ou les aventures d'Agbezuge. Paris: Karthala).
Opland, J. 1983. *Xhosa Oral Poetry.* Cambridge; New York: Cambridge University Press.

——— 1998. *Xhosa Poets and Poetry*. Cape Town: David Philip.

——— 2005. *The Dassie and the Hunter, A South African Meeting*. Scottsville: University of Kwazulu Natal.

Plaatje, S.T. 1930. *Mhudi*. Alice: Lovedale Press.

Pugliese, C. 2006. *Quel est le premier roman gikuyu?* In X. Garnier and A. Ricard (eds.) *L'effet roman: arrivée du roman dans les langues de l'Afrique*. Paris, Université de Paris 13 CENEL: Harmattan, 145–152.

Ricard, A. 2000. *Ebrahim Hussein, Swahili theater and Individualism*. Dar es Salaam: Mkuki na Nyota.

——— 2004. *Languages and Literatures of Africa*. Oxford, Trenton, Cape Town: James Currey, Africa World Press, David Philip.

——— 2005. *La formule Bardey*. Bordeaux: Confluences.

Ricard, A. and F. Veit-Wild (eds.) 2005. *The Oral Written Interface*. Matatu: Rodopi.

Ricoeur, P. 1983. *Temps et récit*. Paris: Le Seuil.

Robert, S. 1991 (1966). *Maisha yangu na baada Miaka Hamsini*. Dar es Salaam: Mkuki na Nyota.

Soyinka, W. 2004. *Climate of Fear*. London: Profile Books.

Sundkler, B. 1949. *Bantu Prophets*. London: Lutterworth Press.

Willan, B. 1984. *Sol Plaatje, A Biography*. Johannesburg: Ravan Press.

LAND AND THE POLITICS OF BELONGING IN AFRICA[1]

Carola Lentz

Land rights and property are 'not about things', as Sally Falk Moore recently summarized, 'but about relationships between and among persons with regard to things' (1998: 33). Rights over land are nested, pertain to different economic and ritual activities (hunting and gathering, harvesting, planting or felling trees, cultivating food crops, sacrifices, building, burials etc.), cover different time spans and differ in territorial reach, ranging from allegedly inalienable 'allodial' ownership of larger village territories, to long-standing heritable proprietorship of family lands and finally to temporary use rights to specific fields. Rights to land are intimately tied to membership in specific communities, be it the nuclear or extended family, the larger descent group (clan), the ethnic group, or, as is the case in modern property regimes, the nation-state. Membership in these groups, however, is not 'a given', as recent studies have shown (cf. Chauveau 2000, Berry 2001, Hammar 2002, Lentz 2002 and 2003a). It is contested. It is negotiable. And, it can change over time.

If claims to land are linked to group membership, the reverse is also true: control over land has been and is still used as a way of defining belonging and, in some parts of Africa, as an instrument to control the labor and/or taxes of those who live on the land. Landlessness may once have been a rewarding strategy for such groups as pastoralists or migrants, but this is no longer the case. In recent African politics, non-territorial strategies of belonging have lost considerable ground (cf. van Dijk 1996, Bierschenk 1997: 29–109, Diallo 2001, Traoré 2002). In most places, one must be able to point to a 'home land' or a 'home village', if he or she wishes to participate in the local decision-making process or be heard in the national political arena. African states, like all modern polities, claim to exercise some form of control over their

[1] This article is an abridged and modified version of my introduction to Kuba and Lentz 2006. I am indebted to Andreas Dafinger, Richard Kuba, Keebet von Benda-Beckmann and Sara Berry for their perceptive comments on the first draft of this text. I also thank the Max Planck Institute for Social Anthropology in Halle which provided me with an excellent working environment when writing-up the text.

national territory. National citizenship therefore implies, at least in principle, the right to reside and participate in the political decision-making process anywhere in the country. However, in many cases this concept of a nation of equal citizens has been challenged by the concept of nations as federations of communities defined by some form of essential 'primordial' membership, such as descent, as, for instance, the recent conflicts in Côte d'Ivoire over the land rights of Burkinabè and internal migrants show (Chauveau 2000, Geschiere and Nyamnjoh 2000). Of course, all definitions of national citizenship invoke notions of descent, but there are differences in the degree to which descent is used to exclude 'strangers' (or, rather, aliens). Furthermore, there are differences in how effective shared national citizenship is for obtaining and distributing rights at the local level. In some cases, the concept of the nation as sharing rights and duties prevails at the national level, while descent-based notions of community dominate the definition of local citizenship (Mamdani 1996). It is within such contexts, which are made even more delicate by a 'scramble for land' and which have also worsened due to demographic pressure and anthropogenic desertification, that the host/stranger or first-comer/late-comer relations have been redefined. Moreover, bureaucratic decentralization and the international debate on the rights of 'indigenous peoples' have contributed to the growing importance of land in the on-going struggles to assert belonging and political rights.

This article will address the issue of land rights, focusing particularly on their political implications. It also calls for a deeply historical perspective. We must not only recognize that today's land rights are negotiable and politically embedded, but also see that this was the case in the pre-colonial—and, of course, colonial—past and that these past configurations of, and conflicts over, land rights feed into current struggles over land and belonging.

The dynamics of 'customary' land tenure

The pre-colonial dynamics of property regimes have received relatively little attention in the recent literature on African land rights. Some policy-oriented studies (cf. Ensminger 1997: 168–170) still seem to share the rather romantic view of pre-colonial land tenure developed by early colonial officials in cooperation with African chiefs. They believed that Africans associate land with a deep religious meaning, that land is held for them in trusteeship by the chiefs and owned communally, and that land is ultimately inalienable. These rather 'naive' (though certainly not innocent) early conceptions of African land tenure, however, were soon revised and refined. By the mid 1940s, Meek (1946: 11–31) presented a quite nuanced picture of 'native systems of tenure' that did justice to the complex web of interlocking communal and individual rights to land, and customary practices of pledging, if not outright 'selling' of land. But Meek, and the anthropologists of his time, continued to think of traditional land tenure in terms of a coherent, homogenous and stable system of rules and beliefs. That Africans could have debated, and held opposing views, about property rights even before the advent of colonial rule, did not even enter the minds of the colonial officers and early scholars.

One of the first substantial critiques of European views of African land tenure was advanced by Paul Bohannan (1963). He argued that indigenous systems, as his study among the Tiv of Nigeria had shown, were the products of a 'folk geography', and not of Western grid-type maps made up of bounded pieces of land, but of a rather flexible, rubber-type map of social relations, characterized by 'short term farm tenure', a system differing radically from Western notions of property. Informed by her research among Central African shifting cultivators, Elizabeth Colson, too, argued that notions of property were conspicuously absent from traditional tenure regimes, at least under conditions of surplus land, and that villages were descent-based, mobile communities, but 'did not claim land' (1971: 202). The idea of communal tenure, understood as 'proprietary ownership' vested in the chiefs, was a colonial 'invention' with highly problematic consequences, Colson insisted (ibid.: 197–198). Later writers have taken Colson's critique of colonial customary law further, arguing that the 'invention' of communal ownership of land, held in trust by the chiefs, was a joint venture between the latter and colonial administrators that furthered the power of the chiefs, as well as their revenues, while also serving European interests in land for state or private use (see, for example, Coquery-Vidrovitch 1982, Chanock 1985, 1991). However, as more recent studies have shown, the colonial codification of 'customary law' did not put an end to debate and conflict, but rather institutionalized unceasing negotiations of and contest over chiefly hierarchies and boundaries of the property-holding communities (cf. Berry 1992, Kuba and Lentz 2006).

Both images of the pre-colonial past—the colonial idea of inalienable, uncontested communal property, held in trust by chiefs or earth priests, as well as Bohannan's and Colson's concept of flexible farm tenure without property rights—are grossly simplified. A number of recent studies have shown that, at least since the early nineteenth century, land in agricultural frontier zones, with emerging cash-crop economies, became more and more highly valued and that land markets developed (even Colson observed this much). These land 'sales' were later, when power constellations changed, sometimes re-interpreted as redeemable pledges or mere leases, but originally they appear to have been intended as outright sales (cf. Amanor 2006, Austin 2006, Boni 2006). Pre-colonial land transactions in West African 'backwater' savanna regions have, so far, received much less attention, but Richard Kuba's and my own findings on the agricultural expansion of segmentary societies in the Black Volta region, for instance, point to the importance the pioneers attached to the material and ritual control of the new territories into which they moved and to a long history of contestation over whether earth shrines, which invest allodial property rights, can be transferred to newcomers or are always to remain the inalienable property of the first-comers (cf. Kuba 2006, Lentz 2006a, also Kuba, Lentz and Werthmann 2001, Kuba and Lentz 2002).

Three basic features of indigenous tenure regimes allowed, and continue to allow, for multiple local interpretations and contestations. The first concerns the boundaries of the property-holding group, or the composition of the 'bundle of owners', as Geisler and Daneker (2000: xiii) aptly put it. Access to land was, and still is, mediated by membership in specific communities or groups whose boundaries were and continue to be notoriously fuzzy. Membership, thus, needs to be negotiated. In many parts of Africa, claiming to belong, by virtue of descent or some other criterion, to the community of pioneers or 'first-comers' to a specific region is the most widespread strategy to legitimate allodial property rights. First-comers are believed to have established a special relationship with the spirits of the land, ensuring fertility and the wellbeing of the community. However, first-comer claims are far from unambiguous. The first issue that presents room for maneuver concerns what is considered to be the 'pivotal historical event' (Murphy and Bledsoe 1987: 124–125) as this determines who is recognized as first-comer: Was it the discovery of the site of the new village, the actual clearing of the bush or some form of conquest? The second issue is the delineation of the territorial and social reach of the group that claims first-comer status. A group may insist on having been the founders of a village, including its various subsequently established sections and satellite settlements. However, the founders of the latter may, in turn, claim to be first-comers in their own right, particularly in relation to even later-comers. The relative chronology of the foundation of settlements can, thus, be manipulated in multiple ways. In addition, first-comer claims can be extended from a single lineage to the entire ethnic group of the lineage.

The second feature of indigenous tenure regimes concerns the fuzzy geographical boundaries of the territories which the property-holding groups claim to own. The kind of boundaries Africans traditionally set has been subject to debate among scholars, but there is consensus that linear boundaries between fields and construction lots were indeed usually marked off, by ditches, paths, hedges of shrubs or marks on trees. By contrast, the nature of the 'borders' of earth-shrine areas or chiefly territories was, and often still is, more difficult to define. When land was plentiful, these territories were probably perceived not as flat homogenous surfaces, but as fields of ritual or political power, with a well-defined center (the shrine or the stool) in the inhabited and regularly cultivated space surrounded by concentric circles of influence, thinning out towards the uncultivated bush or forest which was a zone of contact rather than separation. Where first-comers engaged in hunting, they were interested in controlling rather vast areas and little concerned with fixing boundaries (Ingold 1986: 222–242). Only when more and more bush was cultivated did the boundaries between neighboring territories need to be defined more precisely. In the border zones, the allegiance of houses and fields was usually defined according to which earth priest or chief had originally given the permission to cultivate or build. This process is still going on, and, under increasing population pressure, contains potential for conflict, in which competing interpretations of past land grants and oral agreements are brought into play (cf. Berry 2001).

The third feature, finally, concerns the multiple layers—or 'bundle'—of rights to natural resources. These layers have a socio-spatial dimension, that is, several different persons or groups hold some kind of interest in any given piece of land. And, they have a temporal dimension, namely that the rights may have different 'expiry dates', so to speak, or that some resources are used by different right-holders at different times. In many parts of the West African savanna, for instance, earth priests claim allodial rights to all resources, including farmland, water and uncultivated bush as well as gold or other minerals, lost objects or stray cattle. They assign usufruct rights to villagers and 'strangers', often varying according to the resources in question. It is possible to allow someone to grow annual crops on a field, while at the same time reserving the right to harvest whatever trees there are. Also, earth priests often retain certain rights over water bodies, even though they may have given perennial rights to farm and build on the land around the water. Even in an urban setting, with surveyed and registered building lots, an earth priest may still claim to be ritually responsible for cleansing the earth after a suicide. Again, these bundles of rights are complex and negotiable, and contain numerous opportunities for competition and conflict.

One may ask whether these rights are adequately described in terms of 'property'. Bell (1998) has recently proposed to reserve the concept of 'property' for things that can be alienated and acquired in a market situation, in contrast to resources accessed through membership in social groups. However, such a narrow understanding of property unnecessarily results in the 'othering' of African societies. A wider concept of property, which emphasizes the social and political embeddedness of ownership and allows for a continuum of rights (ranging from mere access to complete alienation) as well as right holders (from individuals to extended families and larger communities), seems more useful (cf. Hann 1998, Lund 2002, von Benda-Beckmann and von Benda-Beckmann 1999). Hobhouse's early elucidation of the minimal conditions under which control over an object becomes 'property', provides a useful starting point: this control 'must in some sort be recognized, in some sort independent of immediate physical enjoyment, and at some point exclusive of control of other persons' (1915: 7, quoted in Ingold 1986: 229), or, in other words: property implies social recognition, long-term control and some kind of exclusivity.

One may also ask whether a focus on property rights does not underestimate the role of violence and relations of power in people's actual access to resources (Ribot and Peluso 2003). Violence, coercion, trickery, material wealth and other 'extra-legal' mechanisms certainly play a role in gaining control over land and other 'natural' resources. However, long-term uninterrupted use of land resources cannot rely on violence and coercion alone, but requires strengthening one's claims to access through building consensus and recognition—i.e. through establishing property (Lund 2002: 12–13). It is important to look at property as a 'bundle of powers', as Katherine Verdery (1998: 161) proposes, but we should also explore the ways in which images of ownership provide 'a vocabulary of legitimation for requests to be made and pressure to be exerted' (Li 1996: 509). In oral cultures, which lack maps, written titles and cadastres, the 'bundles of owners', 'bundles of rights' and territorial boundaries have to be constantly interpreted and reaffirmed through narratives and rituals. Indeed, narratives are central to the constitution of property, as Carol Rose (1994) argues, because they help to build consensus. Yet narratives are also crucial for articulating challenges to existing property rights (Fortmann 1995: 1054).

Even in pre-colonial times, most people could turn to a plurality of authorities in order to have their property claims acknowledged. 'Forum shopping' and 'shopping forums' (von Benda-Beckmann 1981) were certainly more restricted than they are today, but they do seem to have been used. Land seeking late-comers, for instance, had options to 'secede' from one earth priest and approach a neighboring one, if they were dissatisfied with the services of the former. In some areas, new cults or religions, such as Islam, challenged existing spiritual authorities and provided protection that could make it easier for enterprising strong men to engage in novel forms of land transactions. In a nutshell, 'customary' tenure rules and institutions were, and continue to be, subject to multiple interpretations and claims, and are in themselves characterized by legal pluralism. It is evident that the arena became all the more complicated when the colonial (and postcolonial) state entered the scene, creating even more layers of rights, institutions, perceptions, interests and strategies with respect to land.

First-comers and late-comers, natives and strangers

In recent years, discourses on autochthony and 'primary patriotism' (Geschiere and Gugler 1998), i.e. on belonging to a community rooted in a particular territory, have become increasingly important in Africa, particularly the West Africa political arena (cf. Geschiere and Nyamnjoh 2000). In multi-ethnic cities or rural regions with large groups of immigrants, for instance, the democratic principle of one (wo)man one vote, irrespective of specific identities, has often given rise to fears among less numerous 'autochthones' that they could be marginalized

by 'strangers'. Ruling political elites have sometimes exploited such
fears in order to discredit opposition parties, as in Côte d'Ivoire where
the battle cry of 'Ivoirité' became a strategy of political exclusion
(Chauveau 2000, Chauveau and Bobo 2003; on Cameroon, cf. Konings
2001). Discourses of autochthony are also increasingly invoked in the
economic and social arena, mainly to legitimize a firmer control over
land, forest and other natural resources. New programs of community-based natural resource management and registration of collective
rights to land have often challenged the rights of immigrants.

The question of who precisely is 'indigenous', and where, has
given rise to intense debate and negotiation. Sometimes immigrant
groups are unambiguously and consistently defined as 'strangers' by
everybody, including themselves (Chauveau 2006). Here, the debate
concerns the definition of the rights that follow from this categoriza-
tion. In other cases, a long history of immigration and assimilation
of new arrivals produced more subtle and contested distinctions. In
Sefwi Wiawso in Southern Ghana, for instance, the boundaries defining who is a 'real Sefwi' have been redrawn, and defined ever more
narrowly, as the economic stakes of 'autochthony' rose (Boni 2006).
The discourse on autochthony rarely defines the territorial and social
reach of its various claims with much precision. Thus, the home territory and community, where one can claim 'native' status, can be
as narrowly conceived as the village or even the first-comer lineage
within the village, or as widely defined as the chiefdom or the entire
ethnic group. The power of autochthony discourse rests precisely on
the latitude it offers in redefining boundaries according to changing
contexts and interests or, in other words, on its 'combination of stag-
gering plasticity and celebration of seemingly self-evident "natural
givens"' (Geschiere and Nyamnjoh 2000: 448).

According to some authors, the recent flurry in the discourses
of autochthony is an expression of the quest for security and for a
sense of local belonging in response to the global trends of deterritorialization and homogenization. The historical roots of autochthony
discourses, Geschiere and Nyamnjoh argue, lie in the dialectics of the
'liberation' of labor in African capitalism. Plantation and mine owners,
in co-operation with colonial administrators, uprooted migrants from
their traditional ways of life in order to recruit the necessary labor,
while enforcing ethnic classifications and stabilizing home ties for
purposes of tighter control. This 'seesaw...between mobilizing and
homogenizing the labor force on the one hand and formalizing the

difference on the other may help to explain the inherent link between globalization and communalism' (2000: 247). However, as my own research has shown, the boundary between 'natives' and 'strangers' is also drawn in areas where capitalist enterprise played little or no role, and autochthony discourses are not purely of colonial origin, but also arise out of (and transform) pre-colonial configurations of first-comers and late-comers (Lentz 2003a).

Historically, the distinction between first-comers and late-comers served to organize mobility and settlement frontiers (Kopytoff 1987; Chauveau et al. 2004). By (re)defining the frontier as an 'institutional vacuum', the frontiersmen who ventured into uninhabited or scarcely populated areas and sealed a special pact with the spirits of the land, established themselves as 'first-comers' and claimed authority over the land and later immigrants. However, frontiers were seldom completely 'empty', and it depended on the numerical strength and organizational capacities of the previous inhabitants whether they managed to persevere as first-comers in their own right or whether they were displaced, absorbed or relegated to some inferior status by the new immigrants. Once entrenched as 'first-comers', these new frontiersmen had to recruit a critical mass of people to join them in the new settlement in order to cope with an environment of overwhelming insecurity.

A variety of institutional arrangements organized relations between these later immigrants and the first-comers, depending on the numerical strength and degree of cohesion of the former, as well as the political organization of the latter (cf. Colson 1970, Fortes 1975, Shack 1979). In segmentary societies, new arrivals were usually socially and culturally assimilated, and, thus, gradually included in the group of 'autochthones', though the order of arrival was often preserved in collective memory. Alternatively, late-comers were granted their own settlements (cf. Kuba and Lentz 2002). In chiefdoms, shared political allegiance made it less necessary to exert control, and, conversely, achieve access, through cultural assimilation. Here, some immigrant groups maintained, and could even draw considerable prestige, from their status as 'strangers' (cf. Schlottner 2000). In both political settings, however, the incorporation of strangers was not irreversible.

During the colonial period, relations between first-comers and late-comers changed in response to two related developments. Where new opportunities for cash-crop production arose, as for instance on the West African coast, the immigration of 'strangers' took on unprecedented dimensions, partly facilitated by colonial pacification, which generally enhanced mobility. As long as land was abundant, the local chiefs were usually quite willing to accommodate these immigrants, provided they were able to assert themselves as allodial landowners and could extract revenues from the 'strangers'. On the Gold Coast, and elsewhere in their West African colonies, the British generally supported chiefs in their attempts to extend their control over all resources and sometimes even did so by redefining some of the longer-established late-comers as 'strangers', thereby reclassifying them under those who had to pay revenues for land use (cf. Amanor 2006, Austin 2006).

The second development, which transformed relations between first-comers and late-comers, was their increasing politicization. According to the British 'native authorities' model, which was not unlike the French *politique de races*, legitimate political authority was based on shared ethnicity, so that ideally the chief and his subjects belonged to the same ethnic group. But what was to be done in multi-ethnic contexts? Here it was, in principle, necessary to define a particular group as 'natives', who were to be accorded the right to furnish the chief, and the others as 'strangers', who could, at best, be represented by subordinate headmen. In pre-colonial centralized polities, colonial administrators usually acted in keeping with indigenous hierarchies, regardless of whether the African rulers defined themselves as 'first-comers' or as prestigious conquerors who had once come as strangers, but they did establish intimate links between control over land and political authority. In segmentary societies, native status was tied more closely to first-comer status but, not surprisingly, British and French administrators had enormous difficulties in defining precisely where the boundary between 'natives' and 'strangers' lay. In the Northern Territories of the Gold Coast, for instance, the Chief Commissioner eventually settled for the pragmatic definition that everybody whose parents belonged to one of the 'indigenous tribes' of the Northern Territories was a 'native', a definition that provided sufficient leeway for maneuver and interpretation.[2] Colonial administrators, thus, radically simplified matters, at least on paper—and some local actors used this to their advantage in future contestation—, by

---

[2] Northern Territories Land and Native Rights Ordinance, 1931; Public Record Office, London, CO 96/702/7187. See Lentz 2006b: 116–126, 189–197 for examples of such debates from Northern Ghana.

collapsing first- and late-comer status with ethnic boundaries. They were content to attach the label of 'natives' to an entire ethnic group in a given area, and left it to the chiefs and lineage heads to sort out the micro-politics of belonging.

Although these micro-politics were an on-going process, colonial rule did in some ways contribute to the reification of the boundaries between first-comers and late-comers which had been established by the early twentieth century. There were cases in which the most recently incorporated immigrants were redefined as 'strangers', but the reverse, i.e. the conversion of strangers into autochthones that had once been such common practice, rarely occurred. And despite the unwillingness of colonial administrators to become involved in the micro-politics of belonging, competing claimants often tried to enlist their support and thus confronted them with countless conflicting versions of 'tradition' (cf. Berry 1992). The losing parties usually kept temporarily 'defeated' versions alive, and brought them back into play when circumstances changed, for instance, when a new administrator took office or a powerful earth priest or chief died. If native-stranger boundaries were frozen and processes of autochthonization halted, then this ensued from particular local configurations of power. It was not the automatic result of colonial policy, even though the colonial administration was an important source of power.

More recently, the relations between 'autochthones' and immigrants have, in many areas, been affected by the increasing scarcity of land and the conflict-ridden dynamics of the intergenerational transfer of resources. In many cases, it is young men who invoke powerful discourses on 'autochthony', much more so than their fathers, who continue to insist that well-intentioned strangers should not be refused land if they need it for their subsistence (cf. Chauveau 2006, Hagberg 2006). Tension amongst immigrants themselves is also increasing. Particularly the younger generations, who were born in the new environment and shared some of their childhood experiences with the sons of the land-givers, now often claim that they, too, are actually 'sons of the soil' and should enjoy the same rights as 'autochthones'. These young men resent their fathers' subservience and gratitude towards their patrons as much as the latter's attempts to prevent them from planting trees, or freely inheriting or transferring parts of the original land grant (cf. Lentz 2003b). The bitterness of these confrontations often goes beyond that of 'normal' intergenerational conflicts, and is indicative of the changing context in which 'native'-

'stranger' relations are embedded, namely increasing pressure on land as well as returned migrants' growing political awareness.

These tensions also point to the fact that the dividing line between 'strangers' and 'autochthones' is often crosscut by other alliances. Autochthones, for instance, often allocate land to immigrants in order to stake their territorial claims vis-à-vis other family members, lineage segments or neighboring communities. Conversely, immigrants will often support their hosts in such conflicts when this helps them consolidate their own rights to land and their status within the host community. In the periphery of Kumasi, for instance, rich 'strangers' and 'natives' joined together in developing the local infrastructure, as well as holding the chief accountable for the rents and tributes he collected (Berry 2006). In the case of the recent invasion of gold miners in villages in Southwestern Burkina Faso, on the other hand, the immigrants attempted to exploit the cleavages in local communities to further their own cause (Werthmann 2006). Thus, even in the context of increasing competition with regard to land, it is by no means given that this will inevitably result in the exclusion of immigrants.

How relations between 'autochthones' and immigrants actually develop, depends not only on local configurations of power, but also on the larger political context. As mentioned above, colonial governments contributed, on the one hand, to the reification of allodial titles by politicizing the distinction between 'natives' and 'strangers' and generally supporting the property claims of chiefs, but, on the other hand, exercised 'hegemony on a shoe string', as Berry (1992: 345) puts it, and left the micro-politics of belonging largely within the hands of the local communities. The policies of postcolonial governments with regard to the rights of immigrants have been similarly varied. Many West African countries have introduced distinctions between 'national' and 'foreign' migrants, and generally weakened the land rights of non-national migrants, if they have not altogether decided to evict them (cf. Peil 1979, Shack 1979). There are, however, important exceptions. In Côte d'Ivoire, for instance, immigrant farmers from Burkina Faso were strongly encouraged by the state, despite reservations on the part of 'autochthones', because the migrants helped boost the cash-crop economy and were expected to vote for the ruling party. It was only recently that this historic arrangement came under pressure, and gave way to xenophobia 'from above' as well as 'from below', resulting in the expulsion of thousands of Burkinabè and increasing hostility even towards domestic migrants (cf. Chauveau 2000, Chauveau and Bobo 2003). In Ghana and Burkina Faso, immigration from neighboring countries was at best tolerated, but domestic migrants received implicit government support for their claims to land during the 'revolutionary' regimes of Sankara and Rawlings. The latter's dictum that the land should belong to the one who works it encouraged many migrants to denounce the gifts which autochthonous landowners expected as 'exploitation' (cf. Laurent et al. 1994). The argument that national citizens, regardless of their ethnic identity, should have unencumbered access to land throughout the country is still invoked by many migrants and sometimes supported by local government institutions. However, on the whole, the Ghanaian and Burkinabè governments have reverted back towards the recognition of the important role of earth priests and chiefs in the administration of land. The latter are quite cognizant of the authorities and of existing land legislation, and attempt to work the system for their own benefit (cf. Lund 2006). More generally, we can conclude that although African states are often too 'weak' to enforce national land legislation down to the grassroots level, the knowledge that such legislation exists, as well as the possibility for resorting to state authorities or courts for enforcement at certain points, can influence local tenure conflicts, as well as the relations between 'autochthones' and immigrants (cf. Benjaminsen and Lund 2003: 1, 3).

Finally, relations between landowners and immigrants are also shaped by urban elites, urban-based ethno-political associations, and returned migrants who introduce new terminologies into local land disputes (Shipton and Goheen 1992: 311). In Southwestern Burkina Faso, autochthones sometimes form new associations which set down formal rules for land transactions with 'strangers' (Hagberg 2006); in Ghana, even a group of earth priests has formed an association to defend their interests from the chiefs and government (Lund 2006). Land-seeking migrants and their educated relatives have also formed associations to further their interests (cf. Lentz 1995, 2002). Such groups may attempt, for instance, to draw the attention of the national media and even of international NGOs to the violation of 'human rights', while the associations of the 'autochthones' sometimes invoke United Nations discourses on the rights of 'indigenous peoples'.

Land transfers in changing contexts

In African agricultural societies, Shipton and Goheen (1992: 311–312), argue 'unevenly distributed rights in land are adjusted by an infinity of arrangements, often *ad hoc* and sometimes unnamed, for seasonal or longer-term transfers that may include land loans, entrustments, or share contracts'. Obviously, these arrangements can give rise to competing interpretations, particularly in the generation of heirs. Competing heirs may invoke a labor theory of property in order to strengthen their claims to a particular piece of land which they, or their fathers, have worked (cf. Chauveau 2006), while others may call on the idea that village and lineage lands are indivisible and that individual use rights should not be inherited. The questions of who has the authority to transfer rights, and over which parts of a given property, who the legitimate recipients of transferred rights are, the nature of the rights transferred, as well as the temporal dimension of the transfer…—all of these questions must be settled. They become particularly acute when land transfers to 'strangers' are on the increase (cf. Lavigne Delville et al. 2002).

Although there is little evidence for any clear-cut evolutionary trend (cf. Saul 1988, Platteau 1996), there clearly have been changes in the nature of land transfers, particularly in transactions between 'autochthones' and 'strangers'. In order to understand such changes more clearly, we need to disentangle convenient notions such as 'privatization', which has become such a powerful buzz-word in policy discourses, but which actually conflates a variety of potentially contradictory processes (Berry 2006). Three different processes should be distinguished: the individualization of property rights, the commercialization (and monetization) of land transfers, and the formalization of land transactions, by recourse to titles, *petits papiers* or court procedure. These processes may occur jointly, but this is not necessarily so. On the contrary, the more frequently quasi or outright commercial land transactions with 'outsiders' occur, the more often chiefs or earth priests seem to activate dormant allodial rights and challenge the right of individual families to transfer land to third parties without reference to their 'superior' authority (cf. Lund 2006; Berry 2001, chap. 4).

It is difficult to decide whether there is a dominant trend towards increasing individualization of land rights or not. As a number of recent case studies on land transfers suggest, within the confines of the larger property-holding groups, the use rights and rights of inheritance of sub-units (lineage segments as well as individuals), with reference to specific fields or plots, have indeed become more individualized (cf. the case studies in Kuba and Lentz 2006). But the trend is not so clear when it comes to transactions with outsiders, and sometimes spiritual (and material) sanctions against the rights of individuals to transfer land, without consulting the lineage heads and holders of allodial title, are most forcefully invoked.

The picture is similarly unclear regarding the commoditization of land, i.e. the exchange of rights over land for money. In estimating the importance of such transactions, we should also pay attention to the monetization of land rights within families and lineages, where well-connected and well-endowed commercial farmers consolidate their holdings by 'buying' land from poorer relatives and work these transactions under the guise of kinship solidarity. Taken together with the transactions with 'strangers', commercial land transfers seem to have increased considerably, and many authors have attested the development of land markets (cf. Ensminger 1997: 170–175, Lavigne Delville 1998: 119–122, Benjaminsen and Lund 2003, Mathieu et al. 2003). However, there is no straightforward historical development from the 'traditional' prohibition of monetized land transfers to 'modern' land sales. Rather, we find pendulum-like movements, beginning with quite vibrant land markets in some parts of the West African forest belt in the second half of the nineteenth and the beginning of the twentieth centuries, increasing limitations of such transfers under colonial rule, and a re-opening of more or less open commercial transactions since the 1980s and 1990s.

As with individualization, the commercialization of land transfers is multifarious. Although the sums to be paid may be quite specific, the actual rights exchanged are often less precisely defined. The content of the contract may be self-evident to both parties, but as soon as the circumstances change, it must often be renegotiated. In addition, even commercial land transfers are firmly embedded in social relations which specify the conditions and consequences of the transaction. This social embeddedness can be used to the advantage of the politically and economically better positioned party (cf. Hagberg 2006), but it can also provide leverage by which the weaker party may extract additional services and goods (cf. Berry 2006, Peters 2002: 58–59).

That state-led attempts at standardization and formalization of land transfers, through titling programs and the like, have been rather disappointing, is a fact recognized by all scholars (cf. Bruce 1993, Ensminger 1997, Lavigne Delville 1998, Toulmin et al. 2002). The reasons for this failure have been sought in the inadequacies of state land administration (too distant, slow, cumbersome, etc.) and the prohibitive transaction costs of registration, but also in the difficulties of translating the bundles of owners and bundles of rights over tracts of land that are often circumscribed by rather vague boundaries into clear-cut written titles. In addition, corruption and political networking often undermine the formal rules of land transactions, and render state formalization rather 'informal', as Benjaminsen and Lund (2003: 3) have pointed out. By contrast, complex forms of 'informal formalization' (ibid.) have gained increasing popularity in many areas, including contracts between individuals, simply scribbled on sheets of notebook paper; contracts validated by a signature of the customary or administrative authority (*certificats de palabre*); or certificates of land allocation by the chief or the rural council (see Lavigne Delville 2003, Mathieu et al. 2003).

There seems to be an interesting difference in the avenues of 'informal formalization' that predominate in Anglophone and Francophone countries. While the flurry of 'small papers' seems to be characteristic of the latter, people in the former more often resort to the courts (although here, too, land transfers are now often documented, and these documents then presented in court). The difference may be due to differences in administrative and judicial cultures. In any case, taking conflicts over land transfers to court forces defendants and plaintiffs to translate their concepts of ownership of and interests in land in European terms (e.g. allodial title, freehold, leasehold etc.) (Kunbuor 2003). Still, this standardization of customary tenure in the court room (or at the district head's office) does not put an end to debate, on the contrary: courts have become a convenient way of registering and, if initially unsuccessful, 'parking' one's claims, until one day when conditions for reopening the case look more promising. One should, however, be careful not to exaggerate: court cases have proliferated only where the stakes were relatively high and at least one party was wealthy enough to pay a lawyer and take matters to court. In many remote rural areas courts have, so far, rarely intervened in land transactions, and matters only came to the attention of the state authorities when land conflicts coincided with disputes over political boundaries between districts and provinces. Still, even in these 'marginal' areas, the educated relatives of autochthones and migrants have spread an awareness of the necessity of acquiring written arguments, and have, for instance, written local histories or similar documents for future use.

On the whole, there are many examples that point to sustained efforts on the part of 'autochthones', as well as immigrants, to constrain the outright commercialization of land. Part of these efforts is the invocation of the spiritual dangers of 'selling' land, considered detrimental to its fertility and to the community. Similarly important is the introduction of differences in land transfers depending on the use to which the land will be put: many communities are convinced that land may not be refused to a well-intentioned stranger who needs it to survive, but that sufficient land must be reserved for the following generation of one's family, and secondly, that persons intending to cultivate the land or plant trees in order to earn money fall into a different category. These considerations are complemented by debates concerning to which ends, and by whom, money from land transactions may be used. Finally, the vagueness in oral, as well as written, transactions regarding precisely what rights to land have been transferred may well be intentional, on the part of both parties, since it leaves room for future reinterpretation or renegotiation. Whether this embeddedness of land markets slows down or intensifies the commercialization (and/or individualization) of land in the long run, seems to be an open question and may also depend on the future interaction between these markets and new attempts at tenure reform (*gestion des terroirs*, the registration of customary titles, community-based natural resources management, etc.).

*   *   *

Pauline Peters has recently criticized the exaggerated emphasis of the new literature on African land tenure on the negotiability and indeterminacy of land rights, and argues that ambiguity may well 'be a cloak for privilege and class as much as a space for action by the powerless' (2002: 56). She pleads that we investigate 'more carefully how access to land resources intersects with broader processes of socio-economic differentiation and class formation' (ibid.: 59). Her point is valid: questions of power must, indeed, be taken as seriously as the discussion of rights. But class formation through differences in land access seems to be more of a feature of the settler and ex-settler countries of Eastern and Southern Africa than of West Africa (cf. Berry 2002, Cousins 2002). It appears that where rural inequality

in West Africa develops, it does not stem from increasing differentiation between a landless rural proletariat and large landowners, but
rather from the manipulation of 'customary' tenure by urban political elites, investing in commercial agriculture (cf. Konings 1986, Saul
1988, Downs and Reyna 1988, Goheen 1992), and takes the form of
increasingly exclusive boundaries between 'natives' and 'strangers'.
However, the question whether inequality, based on differential access
to land, is really 'on the rise throughout Africa', as Peters (2002: 47)
assures, is far from being settled. Camilla Toulmin, Lavigne Delville
and Samba Traoré (2002: 22) take a stance similar to that of Peters,
but like Peters have difficulties in presenting clear-cut examples which
would support their assumption that weaker groups are, indeed,
systematically denied secure access to land. Much seems to depend
on the specific ecological, economic and political context. In a *longue
durée* perspective on African land tenure, it is the flexibility of people's
relations to land and their adaptability to changing political systems
and economic constraints that are striking rather than clear-cut trends
towards commercialization and/or exclusivity of access. Competing
notions of land ownership and belonging do not seem to be the causes
of strife as such, but can adapt and accommodate multiple demands
made with regard to land and citizenship. In any case, however, we
must bear in mind that land is a special 'substance': it is not increas-
able, non-renewable, and central to both material livelihood and the
politics of belonging.

References

Amanor, K. 2006. *Customary land, mobile labor and alienation in the Eastern Region of
Ghana.* In R. Kuba and C. Lentz (eds.) Land and the Politics of Belonging in West
Africa. Leiden: Brill, 137–159.
Austin, G. 2006. *The political economy of the natural environment in West African history:
Asante and its savanna neighbors in the nineteenth and twentieth centuries.* In R. Kuba
and C. Lentz (eds.) Land and the Politics of Belonging in West Africa. Leiden: Brill,
187–212.
Bell, D. 1998. *The social relations of property and efficiency.* In R.C. Hunt and A. Gilman
(eds.) Property in Economic Context. Lanham: University Press of America, 29–45.
Benjaminsen, T.A. and C. Lund (eds.) 2003. *Securing Land Rights in Africa.* London:
Frank Cass.
Berry, S. 1992. *Hegemony on a shoestring: indirected rule and access to agricultural land,*
Africa 62 (3) 327–355.
—— 2001. *Chiefs Know Their Boundaries: Essays on Property, Power and the Past in Asante,
1896–1996.* Oxford: James Currey.
—— 2002. *Debating the land question in Africa,* Comparative Studies in Society and
History 44, 638–668.

—— 2006. *Privatization and the politics of belonging in West Africa.* In R. Kuba and C. Lentz (eds.) *Land and the Politics of Belonging in West Africa.* Leiden: Brill, 241–263.

Bierschenk, T. 1997. *Die Fulbe Nordbénins. Geschichte, soziale Organisation, Wirtschaftsweise.* Hamburg: Lit-Verlag.

Bohannan, P. 1963. *"Land", "tenure" and land-tenure.* In D. Biebuyck (ed.) African Agrarian Systems. London: Oxford University Press, 101–115.

Boni, St. 2006. *Indigenous blood and foreign labor: the ancestralization of land rights in Sefwi (Ghana).* In R. Kuba and C. Lentz (eds.) Land and the Politics of Belonging in West Africa. Leiden: Brill, 161–185.

Bruce, J.W. 1993. *Do indigenous tenure systems constrain agricultural development.* In T.J. Bassett and D.E. Crummey (eds.) Land in African Agrarian Systems. Madison WI: University of Wisconsin Press, 35–56.

Chanock, M. 1985. *Law, Custom and Social Order: The Colonial Experience in Malawi and Zambia.* Cambridge: Cambridge University Press.

—— 1991. *Paradigms, policies and property: a review of the customary law of land tenure.* In K. Mann and R. Roberts (eds.) Law in Colonial Africa. Portsmouth NH: Heinemann, 61–84.

Chauveau, J.-P. 2000. *Question foncière et construction national en côte d'Ivoire,* Politique Africaine 78, 94–125.

—— 2006. *How does and institution evolve? Land, politics, intergenerational relations and the institution of the tutorat amongst autochthones and immigrants (Gban region, Côte d'Ivoire).* In R. Kuba and C. Lentz (eds.) Land and the Politics of Belonging in West Africa. Leiden: Brill, 213–240.

Chauveau, J.-P. and K.S. Bobo 2003. *La situation de guerre dans l'arène villageoise: un exemple dans le Centre-Ouest ivoirien,* Politique Africaine 89, 12–32.

Chauveau, J.-P., J.-P. Jacob and P.-Y. Le Meur 2004. *L'organisation de la mobilité dans les sociétés rurales du Sud,* Autrepart 30, 3–23.

Colson, E. 1970. *The assimilation of aliens among Zambian Tonga.* In R. Cohen and J. Middleton (eds.) From Tribe to Nation in Africa. Scranton: Chandler, 35–54.

—— 1971. *The impact of the colonial period on the definition of land rights.* In V. Turner (ed.) Colonialism in Africa, 1870–1960, Vol. 3: Profiles of Change: African Society and Colonial Rule. Cambridge: Cambridge University Press, 193–215.

Coquery-Vidrovitch, C. 1982. *Le régime foncier rural en Afrique noire.* In E. Le Bris et al. (eds.) Enjeux fonciers en Afrique noire. Paris: Karthala, 65–84.

Cousins, B. 2002. *Legislating negotiability: tenure reform in post-apartheid South Africa.* In K. Juul and C. Lund (eds.) Negotiating Property in Africa. Portsmouth NH: Heinemann, 67–106.

Diallo, Y. 2001. *Processes and types of pastoral migration in northern Côte d'Ivoire.* In M. de Bruijn and D. Foeken (eds.) Mobile Africa: Changing Patterns of Movement in Africa and Beyond. Leiden: Brill, 153–168.

Downs, R.E. and S.P. Reyna (eds.) 1988. *Land and Society in Contemporary Africa.* Hanover NH: University Press of New England.

Ensminger, J. 1997. *Changing property rights: reconciling formal and informal rights to land in Africa.* In K. Droba et al. (eds.) The Frontiers of the New Institutional Economics. New York: Academic Press, 165–196.

Fortes, M. 1975. *Strangers.* In M. Fortes and S. Patterson (eds.) Studies in African Social Anthropology. London: Academic Press, 229–253.

Fortmann, L. 1995. *Talking claims: discursive strategies in contesting property,* World Development 23, 1053–1063.

Geisler, C. and G. Daneker (eds.) 2000. *Property and Values: Alternatives to Public and Private Ownership.* Washington DC: Island Press.

Geschiere, P. and J. Gugler (eds.) 1998. *The politics of primary patriotism.* Special issue of Africa (68).

Geschiere, P. and F. Nyamnjoh 2000. *Capitalism and autochthony: the seesaw of mobility and belonging,* Public Culture 12, 423–452.

Goheen, M. 1992. *Chiefs, sub-chiefs and local control: negotiations over land, struggles over meaning*, Africa 62, 389–412.

Hagberg, S. 2006. *Money, ritual and the politics of belonging in land transactions in Western Burkina Faso*. In R. Kuba and C. Lentz (eds.) *Land and the Politics of Belonging in West Africa*. Leiden: Brill, 99–118.

Hammar, A. 2002. *The articulation of modes of belonging: competing land claims in Zimbabwe's Northwest*. In K. Juul and C. Lund (eds.) Negotiating Property in Africa. Portsmouth NH: Heinemann, 211–246.

Hann, C.M. 1998. *Introduction: the embeddedness of property*. In C.M. Hann (ed.) Property Relations: Renewing the Anthropological Tradition. Cambridge: Cambridge University Press, 1–47.

Ingold, T. 1986. *The Appropriation of Nature: Essays on Human Ecology and Social Relations.* Manchester: Manchester University Press.

Konings, P. 1986. *The State and Rural Class Formation in Ghana.* London: KPI.

—— 2001. *Mobility and exclusion: conflicts between autochthons and allochthons during political liberalization in Cameroon.* In M. de Bruijn and D. Foeken (eds.) Mobile Africa: Changing Patterns of Movement in Africa and Beyond. Leiden: Brill, 169–194.

Kopytoff, I. 1987. *The internal African frontier: the making of African political culture.* In I. Kopytoff (eds.) *The African Frontier. The Reproduction of Traditional African Societies.* Bloomington IN: Indiana University Press, 3–84.

Kuba, R. 2006. *Spiritual hierarchies and unholy alliances: competing earth priests in a context of migration in Southwestern Burkina Faso.* In R. Kuba and C. Lentz (eds.) Land and the Politics of Belonging in West Africa. Leiden: Brill, 57–76.

Kuba, R. and C. Lentz 2002. *Arrows and earth shrines: towards a history of Dagara expansion in southern Burkina Faso,* Journal of African History 43, 377–406.

—— (eds.) 2006. *Land and the Politics of Belonging in West Africa.* Leiden: Brill.

Kuba, R., C. Lentz and K. Werthmann (eds.) 2001. *Les Dagara et leurs voisins. Histoire de peuplement et relations interethniques au sud-ouest du Burkina Faso.* Frankfurt/M.: Sonderforschungsbereich 268.

Kunbuor, B. 2003. *Multiple layers of land rights and multiple owners: the case of land disputes in the Upper West Region of Ghana.* In F. Kröger and B. Meier (eds.) Ghana's North: Research on Culture, Religion and Politics in Northern Ghanaian Societies. Frankfurt/M.: Peter Lang, 101–128.

Laurent, P.J., P. Mathieu and M. Totté 1994. *Migrations et accès a la terre au Burkina Faso.* Louvain-la-Neuve: CIDEP.

Lavigne Delville, P. (ed.) 1998. *Quelles politiques foncières en Afrique? Réconcilies pratiques, légitimité et légalité.* Paris: Karthala.

—— 2003. *When farmers use "pieces of paper" to record their land transactions in francophone rural Africa: insights into the dynamics of institutional innovation.* In T.A. Benjaminsen and C. Lund (eds.) Securing Land Rights in Africa. London: Frank Cass, 89–108.

—— et al. 2002. *Negotiating Access to Land in West Africa: A Synthesis of Findings from Research on Derived Rights to Land.* London: International Institute for Environment and Development.

Lentz, C. 1995. *Unity for development: youth associations in north-western Ghana*, Africa 65, 395–429.

—— 2002. *Contested boundaries: decentralization and land conflicts in northwestern Ghana,* APAD Bulletin 22, 7–26.

—— 2003a. *'Premiers arrivés' et 'nouveaux-venus'. Discours sur l'autochtonie dans la savane ouest-africaine.* In R. Kuba, C. Lentz and C.N. Somda (eds.) Environnement, histoire du peuplement et relations interethniques au Burkina Faso. Paris: Karthala, 113–134.

—— 2003b. *This is Ghanaian territory: land conflicts on a West African border,* American Ethnologist 30, 273–389.

——— 2006a. *First-comers and late-comers: indigenous theories of land ownership in the West African savanna.* In R. Kuba and C. Lentz (eds.) Land and the Politics of Belonging in West Africa. Leiden: Brill, 35–56.

——— 2006b. *Ethnicity and the Making of History in Northern Ghana.* Edinburgh: Edinburgh University Press.

Li, T.M. 1996. *Images of community: discourse and strategy in property relations,* Development and Change 27, 501–527.

Lund, C. 2002. *Negotiating property institutions on the symbiosis of property and authority in Africa.* In K. Juul and C. Lund (eds.) Negotiating Property in Africa. Portsmouth NH: Heinemann, 11–43.

——— 2006. *Who owns Bolgatanga? A story of inconclusive encounters.* In R. Kuba and C. Lentz (eds.) Land and the Politics of Belonging in West Africa. Leiden: Brill, 77–98.

Mamdani, M. 1996. *Citizen and Subject: Contemporary Africa and the Legacy of Late Colonialism.* Princeton NJ: Princeton University Press.

Mathieu, P., M. Zongo and L. Paré 2003. *Monetary land transactions in western Burkina Faso: commoditisation, papers and ambiguities.* In T.A. Benjaminsen and C. Lund (eds.) Securing Land Rights in Africa. London: Frank Cass, 109–128.

Meek, C.K. 1946. *Land, Law and Custom in the Colonies.* Oxford: Oxford University Press.

Moore, S.F. 1998. *Changing African land tenure: reflections on the capacities of the state,* European Journal of Development Research 10, 33–49.

Murphy, W.P. and C.H. Bledsoe 1987. *Kinship and territory in the history of a Kpelle Chiefdom (Liberia).* In I. Kopytoff (ed.) The African Frontier. The Reproduction of Traditional African Societies. Bloomington IN: Indiana University Press, 121–147.

Peil, M. 1979. *Host reactions: aliens in Ghana.* In W. Shack and E. Skinner (eds.) Strangers in African Societies. Berkeley CA: University of California Press, 123–140.

Peters, P. 2002. *The limits of negotiability: security, equity and class formation in Africa's land systems.* In K. Juul and C. Lund (eds.) Negotiating Property in Africa. Portsmouth NH: Heinemann, 45–66.

Platteau, J.-P. 1996. *The evolutionary theory of land rights as applied to sub-saharan Africa: a critical assessment,* Development and Change 27, 29–86.

Ribot, J. and N. L. Peluso 2003. *A theory of access,* Rural Sociology 68, 153–181.

Rose, C.M. 1994. *Property and Persuasion: Essays on the History,* Theory and Rhetoric of Ownership. Boulder CO: Westview Press.

Saul, M. 1988. *Money and land tenure as factors in farm size differentiation in Burkina Faso.* In R.E. Downs and S.P. Reyna (eds.) Land and Society in Contemporary Africa. Hanover NH: University Press of New England, 243–279.

Schlottner, M. 2000. *We stay and others come and go: identity among the Mamprusi in northern Ghana.* In C. Lentz and P. Nugent (eds.) Ethnicity in Ghana: The Limits of Invention. London: Macmillan, 49–67.

Shack, W.A. 1979. *Introduction.* In W.A. Shack and E.P. Skinner (eds.) Strangers in African Societies. Berkeley CA: University of California Press, 1–17.

Shipton, P. and M. Goheen 1992. *Understanding African land-holding: power, wealth and meaning,* Africa 62 (3) 307–325.

Toulmin, C., P. Lavigne Delville and S. Traone (eds.) 2002. *The Dynamics of Resource Tenure in West Africa.* Oxford: James Currey.

Traoré, S. 2002. *Straying fields: tenure problems for pastoralists in the Ferlo, Senegal.* In C.P. Toulmin, P. Lavigne Delville and S. Traone (eds.) The Dynamics of Resource Tenure in West Africa. Oxford: James Currey, 145–156.

van Dijk, H. (1996). *Land tenure, territoriality and ecological instability: a sahelian case study.* In J. Spiertz and M. Wiber (eds.) The Role of Law in Natural Resource Management. The Hague: VUGA Publishers, 17–45.

Verdery, K. 1998. *Property and power in Transalvania's decollectivization.* In C.M. Hann (ed.) Property Relations: Renewing the Anthropological Tradition. Cambridge: Cambridge University Press, 160–180.

von Benda-Beckmann, K. 1981. *Forum shopping and shopping forums: dispute processing in a Minang Kaban village in West Sumatra*, Journal of Legal Pluralism 19, 117–159.

von Benda-Beckmann, F. and K. 1999. *A functional analysis of property rights with special reference to Indonesia*. In T. van Meijl and F. von Benda-Beckmann (eds.) Property Rights and Economic Development: Land and Natural Resources in Southeast Asia and Oceania. London: Kegan Paul, 15–56.

Werthmann, K. 2006. *Gold diggers, earth priests and district heads: land rights and gold mining in Southwestern Burkina Faso*. In R. Kuba and C. Lentz (eds.) Land and the Politics of Belonging in West Africa. Leiden: Brill, 199–236.

STUDIES IN AFRICAN LIVELIHOODS:
CURRENT ISSUES AND FUTURE PROSPECTS

Leo de Haan

Introduction

In the 1990s, the analysis of poverty in Africa became susceptible to a livelihood approach, with an actor-oriented perspective of putting people at the centre and pointing out their agency in order to explore opportunities and to cope with constraints. It was opposed to earlier structural perspectives concerned with the poverty of dependence and neo-Marxist approaches that depicted the poor as victims of societal constraints. This, of course, does not necessarily mean that the livelihood approach can be set aside as another adherent of the Washington Consensus, with its neo-liberal focus on the regulation of market forces, free choice and individual responsibility. This paper acknowledges that originally the livelihood approach tended to downplay structural constraints especially issues of power, but more recently these issues have been better addressed. However, what remains prominent is the focus of the livelihood approach on agency, i.e. the recognition that Africans create their own history and take an avid interest in their own world of lived experience.

The origin of modern livelihood policy studies can be traced to Chambers and Conway (1992: 9–12), who saw livelihood as the means of gaining a living, including livelihood capabilities, tangible assets, such as stores and resources, and intangible assets, such as claims and access. The first section of this article shows that the approach's popularity is partly due to its enactment by policy circles but also to its roots in various scientific disciplines. Subsequent sections discuss two issues, namely issues of power and multi-local dynamics, which merit particular attention if the approach is to contribute to the understanding of contemporary African livelihoods. In so doing, this article also sets the agenda for future research.

The livelihood approach: modern articulations and disciplinary roots

An actor-oriented perspective challenged the structural perspective on African development of neo-Marxist studies in the 1970s and 1980s for various reasons. First of all, it could not come to terms with the diverging responses of African peasants to the dominant capitalist mode of production. Moreover, studies in peripheral capitalism got caught in a functionalist impasse because they suffered from a continuous obligation to prove the dominance of the capitalist mode of production over non-capitalist modes by the extraction of surplus value through labour and commodities. Also, and despite their wealth of empirical studies, French economic anthropology found difficulties when attempting to make the Marxist concept of mode of production operational in the context of local African communities organized upon the basis of kinship. Thus, the structuralist idea of dominance and surplus extraction proved too schematic when confronted with the deviating behaviour of those thought to be exploited.

In actor-oriented studies a micro-orientation became predominant with a focus upon local households, which was also considered as a convenient unit for the collection of empirical data. As a consequence, various types of household studies appeared in the 1980s. 'New household economics', as opposed to earlier 'peasant economics'—which regarded peasants as passive victims of capitalist exploitation and state dominance—focused instead upon labour, land allocation and income strategies, using micro-economic modelling as an explanatory tool. 'Survival studies', more sociologically inspired, were mainly interested in the micro-social behaviour of poor people in coping with and surviving different types of crises, such as falls in prices, droughts and famines. In those days, both droughts and Structural Adjustment Programmes afflicted Africa. Therefore many of these studies came to rather pessimistic findings, indicating the increased impoverishment of African households, despite their appreciation of people's initiative and actions.

At the beginning of the 1990s more optimistic 'livelihood studies' were undertaken which focused on how people organize their lives rather than on impoverishment itself. One may simply say that, in their optimism, these livelihood studies are an expression of the *Zeitgeist*, but from an inside perspective one could argue that the swing towards optimism was also inspired by the search for more effective poverty—alleviating policies which would put, contrary to top-down interventionist methods, people's daily lives and needs at the centre. The latter point of view is pursued by Solesbury (2003a) in his account of the development of the sustainable livelihoods approach. He argues that the 1987 Brundtland Report, the Greening of Aid Conference at the International Institute for Environment and Development in the same year and the first Human Development Report in 1990, which all called for drastic changes in development policies, must be regarded as the direct predecessors of the 'livelihood founding paper' by Chambers and Conway (1992), in which they established the foundations of a people centred conceptualization of poverty. Subsequently, UNDP (Hoon et al. 1997), Oxfam and CARE adopted this approach

A major stimulus to the popularity of 'sustainable livelihoods' and its further development came with the taking up of office of the New Labour government in the United Kingdom in 1997. According to Solesbury (2003b: 2) the pro-active, self-help image of the sustainable livelihoods approach in improving the lives of the poor fitted very well with the image the new administration wished to project. Sustainable livelihoods became an important theme in the UK's development policy, while the Department for International Development (DFID) initiated a multitude of new research projects and policy debates on the subject. For that reason the Overseas Development Institute (ODI) was able to put a great effort into its popularization among policy makers and practitioners (Carney 1998, Farrington et al. 1999). Also, significant scientific contributions came from the Institute of Development Studies (IDS) in Sussex—especially from the environmental entitlements group, bringing several illustrative cases from Africa on access and institutions to the discussion (Leach et al. 1999)—and from the Overseas Development Group of the University of East Anglia—highlighting the diversification of livelihood activities on the basis of extensive research in East-Africa (Ellis 1998), while also drawing upon earlier work on de-agrarization in Africa by Bryceson (1997) at ASC Leiden.

Finally, the World Bank joined the livelihood mode with its controversial, as well as extremely long, volume *Voices of the Poor* (Narayan et al. 2000), in which again Chambers played a major role.

Generally, these researchers defined livelihood in a similar fashion to Chambers and Conway (1992). However, gradually sustainability was understood more as long-term flexibility and less specifically as ecological soundness, as demonstrated in the second sentence of the following definition.

> A livelihood system comprises the capabilities, assets (including both material and social resources) and activities required for a means of living. A livelihood is sustainable when it can cope with and recover from stresses and shocks and maintain or enhance its capabilities and assets both now and in the future, while not undermining the natural resource base (Carney 1998: 2).

Typically, the sustainable livelihood concept was visualized in so-called frameworks, i.e. schematic figures that tried to imagine livelihoods as a flow of activities going through various boxes representing key elements of the perspective. However, such a framework was

> not intended to depict reality in any specific setting...(but) rather as an analytical structure for coming to grips with the complexity of livelihoods, understanding influences on poverty and identifying where interventions can best be made. The assumption is that people pursue a range of livelihood outcomes (health, income, reduced vulnerability, etc.) by drawing on a range of assets to pursue a variety of activities. The activities they adopt and the way they reinvest in asset-building are driven in part by their own preferences and priorities. However, they are also influenced by the types of vulnerability, including shocks (such as drought), overall trends (in, for instance, resource stocks) and seasonal variations. Options are also determined by the structures (such as the roles of government or of the private sector) and processes (such as institutional, policy and cultural factors), which people face. Their conditions determine their access to assets and livelihood opportunities and the way in which these can be converted into outcomes. In this way, poverty, and the opportunities to escape from it, depends on all of the above (Farrington et al. 1999: 1).

The supportive political environment in the UK, as well as the ample resources made available to research groups and practitioners to develop this method, led to the identification of the livelihood approach as a DFID—instigated phenomenon. However, there is more to note with regard to its popularity, especially the fact that the concept also reverts to well-known and often older approaches from various academic disciplines and, consequently, also became quickly embraced by academic discussions.

(1) Firstly, there is the notion of the 'genre de vie' approach adopted in French geography in the early 20th century to explain ways of life as highly localized, with rooted, stable and socially bounded connections between people and land (Kaag et al. 2004: 51). This notion is still easily recognizable in contemporary human ecology studies of African livelihoods. Striking examples are: environmental studies of soil erosion, desertification, land management and resource competition such as Scoones (1994) on the new directions in African pastoralism; Leach and Mearns' (1996) review of the debate on the African environment; and Tiffin et al. and their (1994) neo-Boserupian study of sustainable agricultural development in the globalization of Machakos, Kenya. A francophone line of descent is clear in studies on man-land dynamics in Sahelian agrarian societies (Raynaut 1997), and pastoral societies (de Bruijn and van Dijk 1995) and the resource competition between both ways of life throughout West Africa (Blanc-Pamard and Boutrais 1994, de Haan 1997).

(2) In addition, Kaag et al. (2004: 51) made it clear that lines of descent are also simple to trace to anthropologists like Evans-Pritchard (1940), who used the term livelihood as a descriptive concept for the strategies of the Nuer for making a living, and subsequently the volume from Kimble (1960) on African lands and livelihoods and the article by Freeman (1975) on the livelihoods of subsistence populations and commercial investments in Kenya.

(3) Moreover, and by contrast to these older geographical and anthropological studies in which 'livelihood' was a simple descriptive term and mainly pointed towards economic activities, the economist Polanyi (1977) came up with a much more sophisticated conceptualization. Drawing upon his earlier work, which also included an account of Dahomey and the slave trade, he not only gave the concept of livelihood more theoretical weight but also considered the economy as socially, culturally and historically embedded. According to him, people need a material base to satisfy their needs and wants, but to understand their livelihoods one has to go beyond the material and thus beyond formalist economics: 'the means not the wants are material' (quoted in Kaag et al. 2004: 51).

(4) Another contemporary academic contribution to the livelihood approach, to some extent also related to previous work in human and political ecology, stems from the first studies on impact of AIDS in Africa, such as of Barnett and Blaikie (1992) in the Rakai district,

Uganda. Within the multidisciplinary field of disaster analysis, Blaikie et al. (1994) further elaborate this livelihood perspective into an access-to-resources model, which proves extremely useful in explaining the livelihoods of poor people and their coping mechanisms in periods of crisis.

(5) Finally, Sen's (1981, 1985) work on entitlements and capabilities must be mentioned. Though he cannot be considered as an early root of livelihood nor, even, as a adherent, Sen is a major fifth source of inspiration to livelihood researchers due to his interest in understanding poverty. For example, Blaikie et al. (1994) partly build upon the entitlements of Sen (1981) as they find that more appropriate for the understanding of effects of disasters than simply 'property'. The views of Sen on wellbeing in terms of capabilities and on entitlements as a process of accessing resources and opportunities stimulated the livelihood approach to better specify livelihood outcomes and access.

Livelihood research in Africa has produced a large number of studies, bringing to the fore the particularities and diversity of African livelihood situations and practices. The communality of the approach is situated in an actor-oriented perspective, predominantly focusing on (poor) individuals and households, aiming at a dynamic and holistic understanding of their actions, i.e. a striving for an integrated complexity of material and non-material objectives, in the context of both local and global opportunities and constraints. What is still lacking, however, first of all, is the revaluation of a political perspective on livelihoods to compensate for the almost imperceptible de-politicizing brought about by neo-Liberal thought. In that respect the conclusion of Guyer and Peters (1987), in their issue on the African household, remains remarkably topical. They not only point towards the fluidity of the household and occurrence of intra-household disparities but, also, made specific reference to a holistic understanding of livelihood and to power relations, which do not feature as prominently in more recent livelihood studies.

> The major shortcoming of structural-functional and economic approaches to the household is the neglect of the role of ideology. The socially specific units that approximate 'households' are best typified not merely as clusters of task-oriented activities that are organized in variable ways, not merely as places to live/eat/work/reproduce, but as sources of identity and social markers. They are located in structures of cultural meaning and differential power (Guyer and Peters 1987: 209).

Secondly, there is a lack of a significant effort to aggregate and generalize findings relating to substantive trends in African livelihoods, such as the phenomenon that, increasingly, Africans tend to perform their livelihood activities in different localities, often quite remote from one another, i.e. the multi-locality of African livelihoods. Both deficiencies will be examined in the remainder of this article.

Politicizing the livelihood approach: issues of power

Access to resources and opportunities are considered a key issue in the conceptualization of the livelihoods of the poor. Nevertheless, for some time now the livelihood approach has shunned power relations in its analysis of access. Some may argue that this has to do with the focus on agency, but on closer inspection, this would appear to be a quite inconsistent reason. After all, agency is embodied in individuals but embedded in social relations, which are governed by institutions in their broadest sense. Therefore, through these social relations, the agency of actors becomes effective and may impact upon structure (de Haan 2000: 349). Power is an indisputable part of social relations and institutions, so the attention on agency is not wholly to blame. The neglect of power relations, and the related over-emphasis on agency—largely that of the poor—, has a lot to do with the somewhat non-ideological stand of the approach. However, now that it has outpaced the constricted structural perspective of the 1970s and 1980s by emphasizing agency, the livelihood approach must also struggle out of the grasp of New Labour and neo-liberal-flavoured policy makers, who have, in their turn, stressed personal responsibilities—even for the poor—in contrast to the prohibitive collective responsibility of the welfare state, while, at the same time, downplaying structural constraints. Therefore, the livelihood approach should now ready itself to integrate power relations more prominently into its conceptualization.

Although the livelihood approach may have adorned itself for some time with the aura of win-win prospects for livelihoods of people, the following is not meant to argue that livelihood is instead a zero-sum game. However, what one should remember is that restricted access to resources and opportunities is the result of mechanisms by which people are purposefully excluded from access so as to maximize the returns of others. Property relations or certain social or physical characteristics, such as race, gender, language ethnicity, origin or religion, are used to legitimize this fencing in and exclusion from opportunities. As a consequence, paying attention to power relations starts with the exploration of the mechanisms and working of institutions, as power relations are legitimized by institutions and continuously reproduced by them—though, at the same time, they may be challenged during their reproduction. Valuable work has been undertaken in this field in Africa by the environmental entitlements group in IDS Sussex. Drawing upon Sen's entitlement approach, which showed that hunger was not a matter of food shortage but, rather, an effect of failed access to available food, they focus upon people's access to natural resources. They start from 'endowments', which refer to the rights and resources people possess. 'Environmental entitlements' refer to the alternative sets of utilities derived from environmental goods and services over which social actors have legitimate effective command and which are instrumental in achieving wellbeing (Leach et al. 1999: 233). Thus, entitlement refers to what people can have, rather than what they should have; the latter being a right. Entitlement comes close in meaning but differs slightly to access in the livelihood approach. This is best demonstrated by looking at the concept of 'mapping'. 'Mapping' refers to how people gain endowments and entitlements; it is the process by which endowments and entitlements are shaped. Thus, in their conception, endowment is the right in principle, entitlement is what one actually obtains and mapping specifies how one obtains it, thus, making power relations apparent.

> There is nothing inherent in a particular…good or service that makes it a priori either an endowment or an entitlement. Instead, the distinction between them depends on the empirical context and on time, within a cyclical process. What are entitlements at one time may, in turn, represent endowments at another time, from which a new set of entitlements may be derived (Leach et al. 1999: 233).

This is illustrated by the example of the gathering of remunerative *Marantaceae* leaves in Ghanaian forests. Before the leaves become endowments, people have to gain rights over them through 'mapping'. This depends on their entitlements: village membership gives collection rights to leaves in commonly owned forests; household membership to leaves on one household's farmland—or through negotiations with other appropriate land-holding families; in forest reserves leaves can be gathered only with an official permit. Women usually first set up a trade in order to finance these permits. Leaf gathering is again a mapping process because of competition among gathering groups of women, and between women within a group, with regard to leaves and sites. Moreover, the mapping also extends to competition with husbands over time spent and other household duties. Once the leaves have become endowments, the entitlements derived from the leaves include direct use, or cash income from their sale. But, before the cash contributes to women's capabilities or wellbeing, a new cycle of endowment and entitlement mapping commences and concentrates upon how it is to be spent. The way the cash is spent is the result of intra-household bargaining arrangements of the women with their husbands and co-wives (Leach et al. 1999: 235–236). What the authors fail to recognize is that, in the mapping process, both individual and collective power processes are at play. Both will be explored further below.

Firstly, gender studies recognized years ago that a neglect of power relations in society would not bring any closer the under-standing of—and solution to—the deprivation of women. Gender studies, therefore, began the analysis of power as the critical mass upon which livelihoods depend and empowerment as the key to the development or well-being. Various notions of power entered the debate, mostly relating to question as to how individuals, as subject to power mechanisms, can also induce change. This is also the focus of a recent study by Lakwo (2006) assessing the latest wave in empow-erment-directed policies in Africa i.e. micro-finance programmes for women, in a quantitative and qualitative analysis of such a case in North Uganda. Following earlier work in gender studies (Villareal 1994: 8–14, but also Kabeer 1994 and Rowlands 1997), he maintains that, in the interaction between individuals, power never completely belongs to one of them. The outcome of the interaction is always the result of negotiation and, herein, power relations are re-created and, thus, constitute a dynamic process of wielding and yielding. The wants of the power wielder are influenced and shaped by the other in the subordinate position. From this point of view, women are not mere victims. They also have an active role in their subordination and can improve their position. Though Lakwo's (2006) quantitative analyses do not show significant increases in the material well-being of the women participating in micro-finance groups, qualitative analysis does indicate, however, significant changes in the power relations between husbands and wives and, thus, has pointed towards empowerment on the individual level.

Secondly, with respect to the collective level of power relations, the work of Bierschenk and Olivier de Sardan (1997, 2003) is extremely useful. In their village studies in various African countries, some of them in the context of political decentralization, they use the concepts of strategic groups and political arenas, which enable us to consider livelihoods as being organized in arenas of conflicting or co-operating actors. Elsewhere, it was summarized as follows: strategic groups are

> groups of differing composition, which present themselves depending on the problem. Sometimes it is an occupational group, sometimes it is a status group like women or youths, sometimes it is a kinship group, sometimes a network of mutual assistance or clients of a patron and sometimes a group of individuals with a common historical trajectory of livelihood strategies. Conflicting interests exist between these groups, which are fought out in local and extra local political arenas.... Depending on their role and activity, individuals belong to different strategic groups and, therefore, the dividing lines between individuals and between groups are never rigid, but variable and fuzzy. In fact, general categories such as 'the poor' do not exist; in the arena of livelihood, inclusion and exclusion may differ in each dimension (de Haan 2000: 352).

In fact, attention for the aggregated effects of livelihood strategies or collective behaviour is still underexposed in the livelihood approach. Justifiably Brons et al. (2005) also arrive at the conclusion that, besides the individual and the household, more attention needs to be directed towards collective behaviour, but in the institutional analysis, power relations are again disregarded

In summary, the livelihood approach would enhance its sense of reality if power relations, as wielding and yielding processes on the micro level and carried out through political arenas at the meso and macro levels, became a standard part of the analysis.

African multi-local livelihood dynamics

The second deficiency in the livelihood approach to be discussed is the relative indifference towards another substantive trend in African livelihoods, namely increased multi-locality. Of course, many livelihood studies point to the importance of migration, but what is meant here is rather the combined effect of individualization, multi-tasking and mobility giving way to livelihood networks. Basically, the concept of migration refers only to the spatial movement of actors. Rather than the movement itself, the resulting interlinking of livelihoods, which actors organize in various places, i.e. the multi-local livelihood network, deserves attention.

Usually households, defined as co-resident groups of persons who share most aspects of consumption drawing on and allocating a common pool of resources, including labour, to ensure their livelihood, are units of analysis of livelihood studies. But, rather than being harmonious entities pursuing an optimal balance as a harmonious domestic unit, African households are groups of individuals also pursuing individual ways to improve their situation. Consequently, there is a trend towards individualized livelihoods, or, at least, towards individual decision-making concerning livelihood opportunities.

Livelihood studies have ascertained that, during the last decade, increasing numbers of people have opted for a pathway characterized by multi-tasking and income diversification. There is a tendency towards livelihood diversification, 'a process by which...households construct an increasingly diverse portfolio of activities and assets in order to survive and to improve their standard of living' (Ellis 2000: 15). Today, few of the African poor derive all their income from just one source, e.g. as wage labour, or hold all their wealth in the form of just one single asset, as the same author also demonstrated in a number of publications on rural poverty in Uganda, Tanzania and Malawi (Ellis and Bahiigwa 2003, Ellis and Mdoe 2003, Ellis et al. 2003). In livelihood studies, diversification in Africa is described as a pervasive and enduring phenomenon, which exists in both the urban and the rural context. Multi-tasking is mentioned as a way to escape poverty, to cope with insecurity or to reduce risk. Note that there is also a parallel to the individualization trend discussed above. Households diversify partly because individual members are able to decide in relative autonomy about the allocation of resources they have access to. Nonetheless, decision making of the household level is still a reality and individual decision-making is understood better within the context of the background of the characteristics of the household people belong to.

Individualization and multi-tasking are joined by a third trend, i.e. the rapid expansion of people's mobility enabled by the improvement of communications technology and transport. Increasing numbers now live on the edge of urban and rural life, commuting from the countryside to the urban centres. Also poor people supplement their income by travelling large distances to earn additional money as temporary migrants. Finally, there is a considerable group of transnational migrants and, in countries such as Morocco, Ghana, Lesotho and Senegal, large groups temporarily or permanently live abroad. No longer is international migration from Africa discussed only in terms of the brain drain and labour extraction. The developmental impact on national, as well as local, levels of both remittances and flows of information generated by migration are increasingly recognized, as is underpinned, for example, in an overview publication on West African migration (Manuh 2005).

However, the relevant issue here is not these impacts as such, but what they mean to the future of African livelihoods. Large numbers of Africans are no longer rooted in one place. Although they maintain relations with their home community, they are also attached to other places. As a consequence, individuals are no longer organized as co-resident groups, i.e. concentrated in space, but resemble individual nodes, connected to each other by livelihood networks, along which flow remittances, information and goods. These multi-local networks of African livelihoods spread like wildfire around the globe. To study the Senegalese brotherhood of the Murids or the Pentecostalists from Ghana as emerging diasporas, trading networks or transnational communities, are all legitimate perspectives. However, they neglect their most distinct and salient feature: they constitute networks of African livelihoods which could constitute an important undercurrent for the strengthening of African development and, therefore, deserve closer scrutiny by a new generation of livelihood studies.

Conclusion

This article argues that a new generation of livelihood studies is needed. It should politicize issues of livelihood by consistently including power relations on individual and meso-macro levels of scale in the analysis. In addition, it should explore the anticipated emergence of a multi-local network of livelihoods, which has gradually begun to replace mono-local African livelihoods. African livelihoods deliver their contribution to the creation of multi-local or even transnational social spaces, i.e. social structures and livelihood practices as configurations of social practices that span places in various countries. The way they use social space reflects their near and remote social relations and their identity. In that sense, a new generation of livelihood studies should also find inspiration in the recent 'spatial turn' in the social sciences in general.

References

Barnett, T. and P. Blaikie 1992. *AIDS in Africa: its present and future impact.* London: Belhaven Press.

Bierschenk, T. and J. Olivier de Sardan 1997. *Local powers and a distant State. In rural Central African Republic,* Journal of Modern African Studies 35 (3) 441–468.

—— 2003. *Power in the village. Rural Benin between democratisation and decentralisation,* Africa 73 (2) 145–173.

Blaikie, P. et al. 1994. *At Risk. Natural hazards, people's vulnerability and disasters.* London: Routledge.

Blanc-Pamard, C. and J. Boutrais 1994. *A la Croisée des Parcours. Pasteurs, éleveurs, cultivateurs.* Paris: ORSTOM Editions.

Brons, J.T. Dietz, A. Niehof and K. Witsenburg 2005. *Collective behaviour as a missing element in the analysis of livelihood vulnerability in less favoured areas.* Unpublished paper. Wageningen.

Bryceson, D. and V. Jamal (eds.) 1997. *Farewell to farms: de-agrarianisation and employment in Africa.* ASC Research Series. Avebury: Ashgate.

Carney, D. (ed.) 1998. *Sustainable rural livelihoods. What contribution can we make?* Department of International Development. Nottingham: Russell Press Ltd.

Chambers, R. and G. Conway 1992. *Sustainable rural livelihoods: practical concepts for the 21st century.* Discussion Paper 296. Brighton: IDS.

de Bruijn, M. and H. Van Dijk 1995. *Arid Ways. Cultural Understandings of Insecurity in Fulbe Society,* Central Mali. Amsterdam: Thela Publishers.

de Haan, L. 1997. *Agiculteurs et Eleveurs au Nord-Bénin. Ecologie et genres de vie.* Paris: Karthala.

—— 2000. *Globalization, localization and sustainable livelihood,* Sociologia Ruralis 40 (3) 339–365.

Ellis, F. 1998. *Survey Article: Household Strategies and Rural Livelihood Diversification,* Journal of Development Studies 35(1): 1–38.

Ellis, F. 2000. *Rural Livelihoods and Diversity in Developing Countries.* Oxford: Oxford University Press.

Ellis, F. and G. Bahiigwa 2003. *Livelihoods and Rural Poverty Reduction in Uganda,* World Development 31 (6) 997–1013.

Ellis, F. and N. Mdoe 2003. *Livelihoods and Rural Poverty Reduction in Tanzania,* World Development 31 (8) 1367–1384.

Ellis, F., M. Kutengule and A. Nyasulu 2003. *Livelihoods and Rural Poverty Reduction in Malawi,* World Development 31 (9) 1495–1510.

Evans-Pritchard, E. 1940. *The Nuer: a description of the modes of livelihood and political institutions of a Nilotic people.* Oxford: Clarendon Press.

Farrington, J. et al. 1999. *Sustainable Livelihoods in Practice. Early Applications of Concepts in Rural Areas.* London: ODI Natural Resources Perspectives 42.

Freeman, D. 1975. *Development Strategies in Dual Economies: a Kenyan example,* African Studies Review 18 (2) 2, 17–33.

Guyer, J. and P. Peters 1987. *Introduction. Conceptualizing the household: issues of theory and policy in Africa,* Development and Change Special Issue 18 (2) 197–214.

Hoon, P., N. Singh and S. Wanmali 1997. *Sustainable livelihoods: concepts, principles and approaches to indicator development*. Paper presented at the workshop Sustainable Livelihood Indicators, Social Development and Poverty Eradication Division. New York: UNDP.

Kaag, M. et al. 2004. *Ways forward in livelihood research*. In D. Kalb, W. Pansters and H. Siebers (eds.) Globalization and Development. Themes and Concepts in Current Research. Dordrecht: Kluwer, 49–74.

Kabeer, N. 1994. *Reversed Realities. Gender Hierarchies in Development Thought*. London: Verso.

Kimble, T. 1960. *Tropical Africa. I. Land and Livelihood. II. Society and Polity*. New York: Twentieth Century Fund.

Lakwo A. 2006. *Micro-finance, rural livelihoods and women's empowerment in Uganda*. Leiden: ASC Research Reports.

Leach, M. and R. Mearns (eds.) 1996. *The Lie of the Land. Challenging received wisdom on the African environment*. London: James Currey.

Leach, M., R. Mearns and I. Scoones 1999. *Environmental Entitlements: Dynamics and Institutions in Community-based Natural Resource Management*, World Development 27 (2) 225–247.

Manuh, T. (ed.) 2005. *At Home in the World? International Migration and Development in Contemporary Ghana and West Africa*. Accra: Sub-Saharan Publishers.

Narayan, D. et al. 2000. *Crying out for Changes. Voices of the Poor*. Washington DC: World Bank.

Polanyi, K. (ed. by H.W. Pearson) 1977. *The Livelihood of Man*. New York: Academic Press.

Raynaut, C. 1997. *Sahels. Diversité et dynamiques des relations sociétiés-nature*. Paris: Karthala.

Rowlands, J. 1997. *Questioning Empowerment. Working with Women in Honduras*. Oxford: Oxfam Publications.

Scoones, I. 1994. *Living with Uncertainty: New Directions in Pastoral Development in Africa*. London: IT Publications.

Sen, A. 1981. *Poverty and Famines. An essay on entitlement and deprivation*. Oxford: Oxford University Press.

—— 1985. *Commodities and Capabilities*. Amsterdam: Elsevier.

Solesbury, W. 2003a. *Sustainable Livelihoods: A Case Study of the Evolution of DFID Policy*. London: ODI.

—— 2003b. *The Sustainable Livelihoods Case Study. Bridging Research and Policy Seminar*. Transcript of presentation 9th October 2003. London: ODI.

Tiffin, M., M. Mortimore and F. Gichuki 1994. *More People, Less Erosion. Environmental Recovery in Kenya*. Chichester, Wiley.

Villareal, M. 1994. *Wielding and Yielding. Power, Subordination and Gender Identity in the Context of a Mexican Development Project*. Wageningen: Wageningen University.

POLITICS, POPULAR CULTURE AND LIVELIHOOD STRATEGIES
AMONG YOUNG MEN IN A NAIROBI SLUM

Bodil Folke Frederiksen

Introduction

For some time, analyses of the social roles of young men in Africa have served to reinforce the widespread pessimism about the future of the continent. Catherine Coquery-Vidrovitch, in a recent article, argues that young people in Africa are disenfranchised as a consequence of a double resistance: from 'tradition' and from those who hold political power (2004: 71). Young people in general have been called a 'lost generation', at the beck and call of warlords and other powerful patrons, and men, in particular, have been characterized as being 'lumpen' elements, violent, ill educated and without morals (O'Brien 1996, Rashid 1997). Photos of boy soldiers and drugged gun-toting teenagers at the back of pickups in Liberia and Sierra Leone have, seemingly, summed the situation up. The present crisis has been understood as one that was embedded in, and accentuated by, the primitive politics and violence of 'failed states,' but rootlessness, of, particularly, young men, has been seen as part of a more general malaise. Social scientists have discussed the influence of mediated global popular culture on young people with regard to the glorification of violence. Whereas there is a general consensus that there is not a straightforward causal chain leading from young soldiers watching Rambo's violent self help activities to their atrocities in the Sierra Leone Civil War, there is still a lingering suspicion that the easy access to global popular culture, in situations of economic decline and political instability, may contribute to the eroding rules of social behavior that were earlier seamlessly passed from generation to generation (O'Brien 1996, Richards 1996: 57–58).

Many of the images and journalistic narratives that have contributed to the panic concerning youth in Africa have come from war-torn nations in West Africa. However, the 'problem of youth' also looms large in East Africa, the part of the African continent where violent conflict and displacement has produced, as well as houses, the majority of refugees, although West Africa is catching up (Zlotnik 1999). Like in West Africa, one element of the problem has been that of 'child soldiers'. In southern Sudan two decades of militarization and violent social and economic upheaval has created a pervasive violent youth sub-culture, in which 'cultural knowledge and the historical experience accumulated by the older generation' has been lost as an outcome of an 'intergenerational gap in communication and a sense among youth that they have lost their political voice' (Jok 2005: 159). In Zambia, generations of young people who were in the vanguard of multiparty politics in the early 1990s experience that political patronage has dried up because of the economic crisis and increasingly turn towards NGOs and religion in pursuit of livelihood and political influence (Hansen 2005). The 'problem of youth' in Kenya, politically fairly stable, has been understood as one of demography and economic development, more than politics. Here, however, I argue that mainstream politics, related to political parties and the state, is an important contributing factor to the marginalization that young people in Kenya experience and resist. The politicians who came into power at independence were already elders, in the classification by Kenyan youth, and they have clung to power and prevented younger generation from influence and access to state resources. Like in Sierra Leone or southern Sudan, young people in Kenya have limited economic possibilities, and no legitimate political voice.

In the 1970s and 1980s, the growth and intensification of economic activities in the informal sector in urban areas were regarded as a possible solution to the problem of youth unemployment and the ensuing social disorder. The issue was often discussed as one of the absorption of multitudes of school leavers within the labour market (King 1977, 1996). Both Kenyans and the international community lacked trust in state institutions in general, and in their ability to solve this problem. Donors and international agencies, while emphasizing 'development' as the route out of poverty, regarded the state as an unreliable partner and were sympathetic toward activities that bypassed state institutions (King 1996: xiii–xiv). As a result, foreign development initiatives and a great deal of international and regional NGO activities were directed towards the informal sector. The case of Kenya, an example of non-socialist development, became important in the international discussion. After a mission of the International Labour Organization in 1972, international agencies and NGOs promoted Kenya's informal sector as an example of self-sustaining capitalist enterprise and profitable employment. *Jua kali* entrepreneurship, as it was called in Kenya, came to play a central role in development policies and intervention, and as a site of hope for young people.

However, events in Kenya in the 1980s and 1990s showed a close connection between economic, social and political development. The state mattered, and its political initiatives had consequences in the most remote areas of Kenya, and among all groups of the population, but especially the poor. After the post-independence one-party state had been abandonned, electoral politics in preparation of the 1992 and 1997 multi-party elections led to the infamous 'ethnic clashes' that displaced large groups of Kalenjin and Gikuyu, and sharpened political antagonism between the opposition and the ruling party, KANU, under President Daniel Arap Moi. Kenya's neighbours also experienced great instability, and refugees flooded into far-away camps and into Nairobi's poor neighbourhoods. A group of young politicians, known as the 'Young Turks,' tried to make headway in politics against the strong opposition of the older generation, firmly in control of the running and finances of the state. They were beaten. As elite politicians, they were far removed from the day-to-day activities of ordinary Kenyans, but the young generation of Kenyans saw their defeat as symptomatic of their own lack of power and influence. They were not so much up against 'tradition' as against the determined, self-interested defence of power and resources, nationally and locally, a defence that exploited widespread anxieties about generational transfer of power. Disenfranchisement and economic decline led to an increase in crime and violence in urban slums and to the recruitment of groups of young men by the 'big men' in politics, particularly into the governing party KANU's militant youth wing (Kagwanja 2005: 81–82). It also led to the emergence of the contested socio-political youth movement, Mungiki.

This was the situation, when I embarked on a study of 'youth culture' in a Nairobi slum in 1995. I wanted to learn about the fate of the multitudes of young men and women, once they had left school, and to study their social aspirations and livelihood strategies within the context of popular cultural practices. My hypothesis was that active participation in an exploding global popular culture might provide new informal economic opportunities for young men and women living in poor urban neighbourhoods, those people that were deemed the simmering threat to stability and order. Mediated and non-mediated popular culture is available to large numbers of young people in

African cities, and activities and enterprises in the popular culture market might contribute to political and economic empowerment, both in terms of making meaning and of making money, as it has done for young women and men in Europe and the US. Furthermore, I wanted to find out if young people participated in politics and saw the state as an institution that acted in their interest. Perhaps the problem of a young generation in crisis had to do with their exclusion from mainstream economic opportunities and peacetime politics, more than them being inherently unruly and violent? For a period of ten years I have followed a group of eight young men in a Nairobi slum, Pumwani, whom I met and worked with in 1995. They called themselves Unity Teens. They assisted me in mapping young people's livelihood strategies, involvement in associational life (sports clubs, community development and religious groupings), and popular culture preferences and activities, using questionnaires, participant observation, life history and group interviews.[1]

In what follows, I shall give a sketch of the location in which the young people made their lives, and summarize some of the findings on their use of popular culture, particularly their use of visual entertainment, in the perspective of their relationship to the state and possibilities of economic and political empowerment. I shall then go on discuss the life trajectories of the group that made up Unity Teens in the context of the changing social and economic environment of an urban slum.[2] I suggest that their cases may show patterns that are general for large groups of well-educated but politically powerless and economically disadvantaged young people.

Location, People and Popular culture

Pumwani is one of the oldest and most interesting areas of Nairobi. Its establishment was the result of the colonial authorities' attempt to solve the problems of housing for Africans in a fast growing capital city. The Municipal Council pulled down older informal African urban

---

[1] Research between 1995 and 2000 was funded by Danida, later I have been supported by Roskilde University. I have benefitted from being a research associate at the Institute of Development Studies, Nairobi Unversity. I thank research assistants Isabel Munandi, David Mita Aluku, George Muoria, Thomas Muinde and Julius Mwaniki.
[2] The research project was called *Youth in Third World Cities.* The present article builds on Frederiksen 1999, 2000, 2002, and fieldwork in 2006.

villages in the 1920s, and many of the residents moved to Pumwani. Among them were a number of women who had migrated from nearby rural areas and now owned property and let rooms. Men from the coast, Muslims, who had worked as safari guides and caretakers for the British, were another core group. Until the 1950s, it was the only area in segregated Nairobi in which Africans were allowed to build on land rented from the Municipality. They built the tin roofed square mud and wattle houses with inner courtyards that are still dominant. From the 1930s to the 1950s, the authorities constructed a number of adjacent estates for their African municipal and government workers, mostly semi detached stone houses that have not undergone much change since then.[3] These houses are still sought after, because of their being cheap and solid. In the 1990s, the government built blocks of flats, known as 'highrise', and, presently, there are plans to demolish the old mud and wattle houses and replace them with new sections of government housing.

Kenya's African-Arab Swahili culture has influenced Pumwani more than any other part of Nairobi. Around 20% of the population is Muslim. The handsome Pumwani Mosque is situated across from the Pumwani Memorial Hall, a low three-winged colonial building from 1923, which contains an Olympic-size boxing ring, a home made gym and a small reading room. Missions, particularly the Anglican Church Mission Society, have left buildings in several places. Amani School of Fashion, Design and Dressmaking looks across at the inhospitable looking colonial beer hall. It is still open, but outclassed by numerous more recent bars and eating houses, most of them more popular than the grim relic from a time when Africans were only allowed to drink bottled beer in supervised spaces.

Communication and intense social interaction are key features of Pumwani. One reason is sheer population density—almost 43,000 people per square kilometer, according to the 1989 census (Onduru and Opondo 1996). Pumwani is close to central Nairobi and serves as a service and entertainment area for the rest of the city. The neighbourhood is famous both for the sale of *miraa* (khat), for good food, for the number of actors, comedians, musicians, and sportspeople it has fostered, and for prostitution, crime and violence. Because of its

---

[3] On the history and present conditions of Pumwani, see Frederiksen 2002, Hake 1977, McVicar 1968, Throup 1987 and White 1990.

long history as an African location, many residents consider the city, rather than a rural area, as their home and invest their energy and resources in urban living. They identify with the neighbourhood's cultural and historical distinctiveness, but also experience discrimination when they move outside. Young people in particular are willing to invest in a better life; many are active in community development and religious activities. They take pride in their community and have kept a spirit of independence.

Both in the colonial period and after independence, overcrowding, lack of infrastructure and absence of amenities have been facts of life. Like in other poor urban areas, the proportion of young people is high. More than one fourth of the total population was under the age of twenty-five in 1989. The continued influx of poor people from the rural areas in the 1970s and 1980s, and again as a result of wars in adjacent countries and instability in Kenya, from 1992 and onwards, have meant that living conditions and security have been deteriorating steadily. It is hard to keep possessions safe, and moving around, especially for women, is risky because of the incidence of violence and rape. Even ordinary everyday work and leisure activities are pursued in a twilight zone between legality and illegality, repression and resistance. Unemployment is high, but most people are extremely creative when it comes to self-employment and a multitude of ways to make money.

Naming of locations, popular culture institutions and styles in the neighbourhood reflect its older and more recent history, and is an indicator of ideals and influences young people live by. The neighbourhood encompasses California, Jericho, Sophia, Soweto, Katanga Base, Beirut and Mogadishu. It borders Burma Market and Kariokor (referring to the First World War Carrier Corps). Congo/Zaire as style and music is ever present. Jamaica is incorporated via Reggae music. The Marley family score high, and wall paintings represent the Reggae singer 'Burning Spear,' named after Jomo Kenyatta in his incarnation as the leader of the Mau Mau. Young people from the core area of Pumwani, Majengo, are scornful of youth from a slightly better off neighbouring estate who preferred Rap music to Reggae—they were *wasofties* or *Babylonis*. Among local football clubs are *Swapo, Amazon, Westham, Atletico Madrid* and *Ohio Sports Club*.

Quite a few of the neighbourhood's bare-footed football players have found their way to Kenya's Premier League. Young people regard football more as a career strategy than as a leisure activity. Both boxing and football were part of colonial and later national community development efforts. Boxers from Pumwani are famous, and boxing has been central to the efforts of slum youth to 'walk upright' and make careers. From the 1980s onwards, boxing has been less popular than *Kung Fu* inspired martial arts, relayed via films from Hong Kong, starring Bruce Lee and Jackie Chan.

In the mid-1990s, most young people in Pumwani were more engaged with video parlours, a fairly new phenomenon, than with politics. These mini-cinemas, with names like *Young Generation Video Show*, were scattered around in bars and family houses of central Pumwani and were sanctuaries and places of inspiration for young people. The parlours constituted a space free of supervision from the older generation, a rarity in the dense and alert neighbourhood. Entrance was cheap, benches wooden, power cuts frequent, roofs leaked in the rainy season, but TV sets screened the latest films that video parlour owners hired in video libraries in central Nairobi. Customers' demands regulated the repertoire. Some video parlours were specialized, like *LA Video Vision*, which showed Indian love films, particularly liked by Muslim women, who were said to pick up enough Hindi to follow the songs and story line. *Fika Upoe* (take rest) video parlour favoured Kung Fu films, and all parlours showed European football. Escape-from-prison films, like *Escape from Alcatraz*, and films about bank robberies, like *Fast Getaway*, were extremely popular. Both robbery and prison life were well known features of everyday life in Pumwani, and audiences enjoyed fantasies of successful escape. The recycling of these narratives expressed the low-intensity but persistent resistance against state control and the rule of law. The dangers inherent in some of the foreign shows included the learning of fighting techniques and 'how guns are handled.' On the positive side, customers reckoned that video parlours provided education about other countries, 'not Kenya,' and kept teenagers away from the streets. A young man stated that watching the shows 'occupies my time, hence I am not aimlessly wandering around and being harassed by the police,' and an older customer expressed a common view: 'The youth get general information on how to go about their life, but also bad knowledge, e.g. free love.' Pornographic movies, shown late at night, were a much criticized feature of the video repertoire.

The police and 'thugs' provided real life excitement, as the latter would often seek refuge in video parlours when fleeing, or so the police claimed, and customers and owners had to pay bribes to be

allowed to carry on with the shows. Video parlours, like other enterprises that have managed to accumulate and attract a little wealth,
have been a resource for ill paid police officers to tap into. As a result
of this, and of reliance upon customers with uncertain incomes, the
video parlour market has been unstable—some parlours were in business only for a few months before their owner decided to use the
premises for other activities.

Young men formed the greater part of the audience; it was not
considered suitable for young women to frequent video shows, and
they faced the risk of being raped when they left the cinemas, mostly
situated in a part of Majengo 'where people don't sleep,' and walked
home after dark. Only 'toughened up women go,' one male respondent
told us; but this was contradicted by the young women themselves.
One told that she would go to video cinemas twice a month, but she
would do so 'with fear.'

The favourite genres and mixed attitudes to popular films were similar to those of young people in Amaoti, an informal township outside
Durban, in a survey carried out by Preben Kaarsholm, and in Sierra
Leone, in one by Paul Richards (Kaarsholm 2006: 157–159, Richards
1996: 105–111). The young people who made up Richards' sample in
1993–1994 engaged with the state and political power in a context
of violence that was formed by the specific politics of Sierra Leone
and Liberia.[4] In Amaoti, a few years after South Africa's democratic
transition, there was a strong alternative moral discourse, strongly
influence by the state, urging young people to find respectability
'through education, religious activity, cultural group involvement or
political work' (Kaarsholm 2006: 159). In Pumwani religious institutions and NGOs promoted similar aims, but in contrast to Amaoti they
did not encourage 'politics' as a respectable activity. In all cases, the
video shows were regarded as being both 'educative' and corrupting:
learning from Rambo how to act on one's own, seeing how to 'handle
guns,' getting to know about 'love' in foreign surroundings were both
good and bad.

Video cinemas did not screen the local TV shows that were among
the most popular items on television. TV sets were available in many
dwellings in spite of the lack of other facilities. *Vitimbi* and *Vioja*

---

[4] See Africa Development 1997, 22 (4–5) for a discussion of Richards' findings and
more generally the sources of youth politics in Sierra Leone.

Mahakamani are sitcoms in Swahili, partly located in Pumwani, and feature local stars. They represent the good-humoured way people in the slums (are supposed to) go about their daily lives, and were enjoyed for the recognition and good laughs they provide. We were told that *Vitimbi* 'has a teaching message,' and one young woman explained that she would watch *Vioja* with her illiterate mother, and use the narratives of family conflicts and their resolution to reflect and discuss her own family problems.

The foreign shows were central for young people. The high profile stars were household names, referred to as one refers to friends or real-life famous Kenya figures. In 1995 everybody talked about *Fresh Prince of Bel Air*. Will Smith alias 'Fresh Prince,' the successful young black rapper and comedian, was *the* narrative with which young men's own life stories and career dreams would resonate, and which women would adore. In 1997 *The Bold and the Beautiful* was the top show among young women. They admired Stephanie, the matriarch of the series, for trying to hold her family together. She was the one role model young women named after discussion and dismissal of other possibilities, including mothers, teachers and national politicians. They saw Stephanie as a strong and independent woman of the sort that was increasingly being beamed from the West via media narratives, and the world of global institutions, like the UN and local women's organizations, which both contributed to the dissemination of ideas of gender equality. 'Now we have *Beijing*,' referring to the United Nation's Women's Decade, was widely used as shorthand for the ongoing transformation of gender relations which was no secret to young people in Pumwani. *The Bold and the Beautiful* unfolds around a fashion firm, an added attraction. Fashion and design were constant preoccupations with the young set in Pumwani, both because of real or dreamed of income opportunities—sale of fashion clothes, second-hand or locally tailored after designer models—and for the opportunity that dressing stylishly offered of projecting in public who they are.

Young people's distinctions in the area of popular culture added up to a pattern that showed a preference for popular culture from the South and from the US. In a mental map of music, African America and Congo/Zaire loomed large, followed by Jamaica, South Africa and other African countries. In sports USA, Brazil and Nigeria predominated. Young men and women valued black American music, sit-coms and styles of dressing and interaction because of an atmosphere of irreverence and subdued or open anger and sorrow. Reggae travels well, and young people regarded it as a genre that is local, Jamaican and South African at the same time. Young musicians performed and recorded Rap music in Kiswahili. Although the greatest Lingala-Soukous stars were known to come from Congo/Zaire, the style and language have been appropriated in Kenya to the extent that the genre was regarded as indigenous. Local Kenyan stars and styles—themselves products of global cultural interaction—were prominent in music videos, live concerts and on cassettes. US, India and South East Asia provided the most popular visual culture. A pride in Kenyan popular culture practices did not entail a strong identification with Kenya as a nation. Being African was commonly valued more than being Kenyan.

Unity Teens 1995-2006: From Popular Culture and the Informal Sector to NGOs, Religion and Migration

The mid-1990s saw the height of the KANU government's domination. The militant wing of the party, the KANU Youth Wing, controlled many aspects of political and social activities in Pumwani in cahoots with the local police. They defended the privileges of their paymasters, the older generation within the ruling party (Kagwanja 2005: 91). This axis did not contribute towards reducing crime and making the neighbourhood secure. For most young people the involvement in popular culture practices occurred in a tension with their own experienced lack of resources and prospects. The majority lived in congested mud houses with no privacy or in tiny 'cubes,' rooms added on to pre-existing buildings, often belonging to parents; water had to be fetched at crowded public taps, electricity was teased into houses illegally, and very few institutions had a real interest in the situation of youth. The church, the mosque and a few NGOs were exceptions. The government was strong in rhetoric, referring to youth as 'the future leaders of the nation,' which was appreciated, but also seen as slightly bewildering by the young people living in the limbo of an urban slum. The residents of Pumwani, like other Kenyans, lived their daily lives in an atmosphere of political repression and lack of human rights. They associated politics with corruption and the use of force. The common view was, the less politics the better, although the famous Kamukunji grounds, used for political rallies, is part of the neighbourhood, and Pumwani was regarded as an opposition zone.

When I began fieldwork on youth culture in the mid-1990s, my key informants and research assistants were Julius, George, Eric, Thomas, Patrick, Nixon, Gabriel and David Mita. They formed the group called 'Unity Teens'. The name was a gesture towards both Kenyan politics, as they were then, and western ideas of what it is to be a young person. Julius and George, brothers then in their twenties, lived in Majengo, the core area of Pumwani. Living in the centre rather than the 'sub-urbs' of the neighbourhood, was a source of satisfaction: 'people from Majengo are more civilized or advanced in life.' Both brothers were active Christians and lived in rooms they had built in connection with their mother's house. They ran a barber shop named *Soul Brothers.* The shop operated from a wooden structure in front of the house and faced one of Pumwani's busy streets. With his friend Eric, Julius also rented a second-hand clothes stall in Gikomba, a nearby informal market, and he travelled to Tanzania occasionally to buy wholesale. The stall was named after a popular TV sitcom, *Fresh Prince of Bel Air,* featuring the African American actor Will Smith—a cultural hero among the young in Pumwani, at the time.

Thomas, jokingly nick-named Isiah by himself after the popular US basket ball player Isiah Thomas, whose looks and 'NBA' hair and dressing style he emulated, lived near Pumwani Mosque with his mother and siblings, in the predominantly Muslim part of Pumwani called *Katanga Base.* He was a Catholic, active in the choir of a local church. His grandfather had been with the King's African Rifles in Burma during the Second World War. Like Julius and Eric, he sold second-hand clothes that he picked up in Mombasa, worked for an advertising agency, and wanted to work with computers. He was hoping to migrate to the U.K.

David Mita was an artist. His father and grandfather were tailors and had migrated from western Kenya. He had an unusual talent for dancing, acrobatics, design and drawing, and wanted to make a career as a cartoonist (*Tin Tin* and *Asterix* were the models). For a while, he was sponsored by a foreign NGO to go to art school. He started out his career as a performer and musician with Gabriel. Together, they formed a duo. Later, after Gabriel had been 'born-again' and decided to follow his religious calling, David formed *Group Africa,* a song and dance group in the *soukous* music style with three other young men, one of them Gabriel's younger brother. The group performed to taped music as they could not afford instruments. In order to meet the demand for the particular Congolese form of performance, the group members had learnt some Lingala, a *lingua franca* of Congo/Zaire, in addition to the other three languages which they spoke. They acquired their linguistic and dance skills partly from watching Zairian music videos, partly from a Pumwani business enterprise which specialized in teaching performance-related skills, hiring out sound equipment to discos, and which also had a video cinema on its modest premises. David designed the extravagant costumes for the group. They had to change outfits two or three times during every performance in order 'not to disappoint our followers.'

Julius, Eric, George, Thomas, Gabriel, Nixon, Patrick and David Mita were all firmly located in the physical and social space of Pumwani. They constituted a dynamic social group, held together by shared understandings of values and meanings. Their lives and ideas were embedded in life-styles and narratives from the larger world, which were received, contested and became meaningful to them. Popular culture practices were more central to this group than to their parents and grandparents. However, they upheld other social distinctions more carefully than those to do with popular culture: generation, education, class, religion and rural or urban orientation were all central to social interaction and identity. According to the young men, ethnic difference did not matter in the mixed social space of Pumwani. 'Tribe is for older people,' they told me. It was also associated with formal politics and support of political parties. From observation, however, it was clear that ethnicity as a resource more than as a limitation was an element in the complex of social identities that made up the characteristics of groups and formed their life perspectives. Young people like Unity Teens, who strove to lead respectable lives, regarded the young men who did participate in politics, like KANU youth wingers, as anti-social and semi-criminal elements—in fact 'lumpen'. They regarded the authorities as a hindrance to business, and state agencies made political participation difficult.

Pumwani has not changed radically in the ten-year period since 1995, and it still shares its defining structural characteristics with thousands of urban spaces in sub-Saharan Africa: lack of infrastructure, poverty, crime, unemployment, unhealthy housing, high population density and insecurity. Kenya has had a significant change of government in 2002, when KANU was defeated, and some changes have reached Pumwani. Primary schooling is more affordable than under the previous regime. Matatus and buses are fewer but more safe. Roads are better, and at night, security lights cast their glare from strategically placed masts over the surroundings, a response to rising crime rates and increased violence. Most video parlours have closed because of insecurity. Some families have moved into the new 'highrise' flats in the face of opposition from locals whose houses have been pulled down, but who cannot afford the higher rent. They have had to move to slum areas that are further away and have even less infrastructure.

The new government has not meant that a new generation has entered politics. Prime Minister Mwai Kibaki is a member of the old guard, which has dominated Kenyan politics since independence, and keeps up a level of control that is seldom challenged. Eric explains:

> Politics in Kenya is something like a monarchy. I believe that the first government and the people who are in the government today are just the same persons used to be before. We youth are not given the chance...If we vote we just vote for the same people who used to be there.... The national cake is just eaten by one family—I mean the monarchs.

Julius agrees:

> This government is not better than the other one. This government has corruption and it is very open. The big fish are not arrested or affected even if they are found guilty of any offence. This issue of promising young people some jobs: instead of giving us jobs they have taken away jobs young people used to do like the matatu business. These young guys have nowhere to go, they resort to doing crimes like mugging etc. Many young people are used in riots by the big people, the parliamentarians, the MPs, the councillors. They take the local brew, which is cheap, then they become drunk and cause some havoc to the neighbourhood.... They are paid maybe a hundred shillings, and when you get injured they are not there for the medical service, you will cater for yourself.[5]

His words echo those of a young teacher in Gulu, discussing the marginalization felt by young people in northern Uganda and their partial acceptance of the violent rebel movement, The Lord's Resistance Army:

> The youths are used, highly used, and because they are poor... they are easily manipulated.... Elders capture power all the time, and they make use of youth in many ways, but all the time it is not for positive

---

[5] Interviews Pumwani, August 2006.

aspects; all the time for something that causes friction in society (Finnström 2006: 213).

According to him, an important element in the appeal of the rebel movement is that they side with young people in the area in their resistance against the state.

Young people did not have any expectation of being assisted or empowered by the state in 1995—nor do they now, ten years later. In the mid-1990s, young people in Pumwani were preoccupied with obtaining the national ID card and a passport. Although Kenyan citizens are entitled to both, and non-production of ID cards when accosted by police, meant harassment and arrest, obtaining the documents was cumbersome and expensive. Bribes and endless delays were routine. In 2006, registration of voters for the 2007 election was underway. The expectation was that almost a million and a half young voters will not be registered. Members of KANU, now in opposition, complained that the present government, like the previous one, is unwilling to issue ID cards and register voters in areas known to be sympathetic to the opposition (*Sunday Nation*, 13 August 2006). In addition, it is often difficult or impossible for young people from poor families to get hold of the adequate documents to prove their identity—parents' marriage licences or their own birth certificates. The result is that poverty prevents young people from participation in formal politics. The Mungiki social movement is one of the outlets for young people. They were involved in the 2001 post-election 'matatu wars', where large groups of young men lost their livelihoods. Followers have made their presence felt in the poor neighbourhoods of Nairobi, including Pumwani, but the violence of members, and what is seen as their outdated ethnic identification with Gikuyu political tribalism, make them both dangerous and irrelevant to young people whose outlook is global and whose ambition is to be upwardly mobile.[6] Like those who are hired by politicians, they are also regarded as self-serving and 'lumpen.'

The popular culture scene has changed in accordance with local and global trends—it is still very important for young people and even more accessible than it was in the 1990s. Internet and mobile phones have made their appearance, and their availability may create a second wave of empowerment for young people. The most popular

---

[6] On Mungiki see Kagwanja 2005, particularly pp. 201–205.

soap operas now come from Mexico and the Philippines, but Kenyan shows still have large audiences. In 2006 many young men and women in Pumwani debated the social and moral issues emerging from the story-lines in *Mukatano Junction*, a drama series set in a fictitious village, dealing with everyday conflicts and issues, such as 'malaria prevention, safe sex, parental involvement in schools and how to look after donkeys'.[7] The series is written and produced by Kenyans and supported by the British development agency, DFID. Five million people watched the thirteen first episodes.

The young men who used to call themselves 'Unity Teens' were all unmarried in the mid-1990s and on the threshold of careers. Now, they are married, formally or informally, and four of the eight have moved out to the slum. They are no longer preoccupied with popular culture, a characteristic of youth. None of the eight chose illegal activities as a livelihood, but many of their friends of similar age have. Guns are cheap in Pumwani and adjacent Eastleigh. Drugs are rampant and a new influx of migrants from rural areas and refugees from centres of unrest contributes both to instability and to new livelihood opportunities. For young men crime is one of the flourishing but also high-risk livelihood opportunities. Insecurity affects the daily lives of every inhabitant in Pumwani. David Mita explains:

> Young guys in the community are dying, most young people are being shot...it is an issue of drug abuse and politics, because some of them are being given money to go and buy drugs, so that they can stand up and start maybe shouting and go and shoot people and hijack. So they are being used, it is a political issue, they are given money because of the poverty in the community.[8]

The young men from Pumwani have all seized opportunities bound up with the openings that the environment of neo-liberalism offers a growing middle class, as well as marginalized populations of the great African cities. The informal sector is still an important career trajectory, and skills and innovations learnt from popular culture can make a difference in the competitive environment. Some have been successful, but most have run into the dead ends that are the

---

[7] Http://www.dfid.gov.uk/casestudies/files/africa/east-africa-tv.asp (accessed October 5, 2006).
[8] Interview Pumwani, August 2006.

consequence of increasing poverty and competition. Mita describes the situation:

> The competition is what makes us develop, though we have some problems with young guys not having jobs, university students not knowing where to go—they are just there. Most of the people are in *jua kali*. What is remaining is, you come up with a creative idea to start a business. But people are now like lions, they just wait for you. If you start a business the person just takes the business and implements the same business … so maybe if you are selling something for two shillings the other person will sell at one shilling, so that he can overdo you.[9]

NGOs, migration and religious institutions are all growth sectors. Politics, on the other hand, is not regarded as a profitable area. NGOs provide some support and opportunities for young people, but in terms of stability and long-term perspectives they are even less secure than the informal sector. They also pay less. They offer ample opportunity for courses, capacity building and skills development, but very little paid work. Many of their activities have a paternalist flavour: they deal with young people as target groups rather than as responsible equals. There is a good deal of competition between NGOs for the clients they depend on in order to generate funds from national or foreign donors. The major NGOs in Pumwani aim their activities at the same groups of unemployed and marginal young people and offer very similar activities to improve health, combat HIV/AIDS, train skills and entrepreneurship so as to manage micro businesses.

Because of international panic over the 'problem of youth,' young people are central objects of intervention. An implicit purpose of NGO activities is to keep them away from pursuits that they enjoy, but that are regarded as a threat to themselves and the community. Mita has been working for NGOs for more than ten years—he is now provided with a monthly allowance by one, but not a real salary. He tells of the frustrations of working with the mobilization of young people:

> I joined a NGO. The challenge that I had in the organization was that my boss used to change me from this programme to this programme; she saw that I had some skills and some creativity and wanted me to inject in new programmes and uplift new programmes. But the problem was that when I moved from a programme the programme collapsed, so I felt we were wasting programmes.[10]

---

[9] Interview Pumwani, August 2006.
[10] Interview Pumwani, August 2006.

The common perception in Pumwani is that the only people who really benefit from the NGOs are those who own or are employed by them. They are free floating institutions—not accountable to agencies that are accessible to the people involved in them.

Islam and Christianity have long histories in the area. The Pumwani Mosque and the Muslim community have provided prescriptions for living and welfare support networks for those in need, for over sixty years. During the 1950s a number of Gikuyu, who were the backbone of opposition to the colonial government, converted to Islam and took on new names and identities in order not to be recognized by the authorities (Kagwanja 2005: 95–96). Islam has provided respectability and protection for women, often single, who found themselves alone in urban areas (Obbo 1980). Christian missions have also looked out for the marginalized. Their primary concern has been with evangelism and the creation of an educated work force. They have organized informal education, training programmes and charity activities since the 1940s. The Christian Industrial Training Centre and St. Johns Community Centre, next to each other on the outskirts of Majengo, are the most prominent ones. St. Johns was established in 1947, as a response to the social crisis that rural immigration into Nairobi had constituted.

The charismatic revival within the established churches as well as the foundation of new Pentecostal churches have led to an intensification of religious life, and ensuing economic and education activities. Christian churches experience increasing competition with Islam, and Muslim and Christian 'crusades' are frequent in the neighbourhood. Young people benefit in several ways. Some young men from Christian backgrounds, who do not have the means to get married within their own community, convert to Islam because the economic demands in connection with Muslim marriage are not so high. However, conversion is a big decision, we were told: elders in the Muslim community make sure that once you have converted it is for life.

Migration is still regarded as the golden road to success, kept alive by the never-ending stream of images and sounds from parts of the world where young, dynamic people do not have to rely on the fragile and uncertain life opportunities that are increasingly the only option for those in poor urban areas of Africa. It is kept alive also by the young people who do manage to migrate, often students, and send home remittances and return for visits. Most have far better living standards than those left behind.

Conclusion

Unity Teens, now adult, have all, in different ways, exploited both established and new livelihood opportunities. Patrick has graduated from college and found employment in a national IT firm. He now lives with his wife in a middle class area of Nairobi. Nixon had to drop out of further education, in order to look after his younger siblings, when his mother was no longer capable of doing so, because of illness. He lives in Pumwani and is still hoping to re-enter college and finish his education. With his wife and daughter, Eric has settled in Kibera at the opposite end of the city—a huge Soweto type settlement, which houses both poor and middle class people. He looks after his uncle's photo copying business, and has expanded it with the sale of second-hand textbooks for schools. Gabriel has disappeared from the horizon of the rest of the young men. They know that he has become an itinerant preacher, connected to one of the charismatic churches, after having been 'born again,' as have many of his contemporaries and elders.

Thomas has succeeded in migrating to Great Britain, with the assistance of family members living there. He is pursuing business studies and has settled in London with his wife and child. His younger brother has a BA degree from Nairobi University, also in business studies, and hopes to join him. George and Julius still live with their mother in the family house in Pumwani. Julius gets monthly rent income from a house he has built of iron sheets in a fast growing suburb of Nairobi. Together, the two brothers undertake a number of informal activities: they run their barber shop, sell second hand clothing and get infrequent jobs in health and human rights campaigns, conducted by a local Christian NGO. They both have wives and children. Their wives add to the family's income when they can, by selling fruit and vegetables locally, in small quantities and with little profit.

David Mita lives in a small, airless room, close to George and Julius, with his wife and two children. He wants to be a movie director, and struggles to make use of his artistic and pedagogic talents in the service of a competitive, secular NGO. His wife, Farida, is an orphan and, like most other young people, she and David get no significant help from their families. Rent is cheap, but provision of food and payment of school fees leaves no room for emergencies such as medical bills or visits to relatives in rural areas.

Based on their experience with the limited possibilities of expansion in the informal sector, young men, in particular, explore new livelihood strategies, most importantly, migration, participation in the politics and business opportunities of NGOs and religious institutions. These activities bypass the state, as advocated by donors and NGOs in the 1970s and 1980s. NGOs provide issue-oriented politics, religion offers moral certainty. Their references are to global institutions and agendas—the great world religions and universal human rights. As a result, the young people who have been the subject of this essay know the local state only in its control functions. They do not get the knowledge and experience of democratic politics and state institutions that might be channelled into pressure for reforms. Countless similarly positioned young men and women in African cities pursue the same strategies. The lack of serious, self-confident engagement with local politics and the state is one of the serious problems for young educated people in Africa, rather than influence from the media and participation in popular culture.

Expectations of easy mobility in the wider world, outside the known community of the slums, have been obliterated by the grim and ever shifting reality of a society in economic and political crisis. The repressive politics of the Kenyan state has fed into an economic situation, characterized by retrenchment of public sector jobs and few chances of entry by young people into the formal private or public sector. However, Julius, George, David and Nixon still dream of moving out of Pumwani, as summed up by Nixon in 1995:

> Me, I see myself somewhere in the United States. Somewhere like Michigan State. But it is just a big dream. And also there are some small steps which I need to seriously embark on, like uplifting my family's financial position, and also for myself I need to go to college, get a good paying job, and then I fly off.

Mita's wife, Farida, a talented and energetic young woman, wants to hire a market stall in central Nairobi where she can sell her own handicraft products—crochet tablemats that she has learnt to make at a course at a local NGO. What she would really like is to be a dancer, but her dreams recede into the horizon. She planned to work in Norway or Sweden for a period, and then return to Pumwani, 'to show what I have achieved.' None of them despair, but their aspirations of social mobility have, on the whole, not been fulfilled. Eric expresses their hopes and resignations, in 2006: 'Life is not the way I used to say it would be. We used to be told since we were young, "one day we shall be future leaders." But things change. I am still big, but I am not a leader." Julius adds,

> So, I, myself, believe in the saying 'Hujafa hujumbika', which means that 'You are not dead, creation still goes on.' That gives me hope in life...So I still hope that one day I will be someone, maybe I will expand in business and I will become someone prominent. I'll have a good life thereafter.

References

Coquery-Vidrovitch, C. 2004. *Femmes et jeunes en ville: nouveaux acteurs en Afrique occidentale*. In A. Triulzi and M.C. Ercolessi (eds.) State, Power and New Political Actors in Postcolonial Africa. Milano: Feltrinelli Editore Milano, 67–86.

Finnström, S. 2006. *Meaningful Rebels? Young Adult Perceptions of The Lord's Resistance Movement/Army in Uganda*. In C. Christiansen, M. Utas and H.E. Vigh (eds.) Navigating Youth, Generating Adulthood. Uppsala: Nordiska Afrikainstituttet, 203–227.

Frederiksen, B.F. 1999. *'We Need that Life'. Global Narratives and Local Aspirations among Youth in a Nairobi Slum*. In N.N. Sørensen (ed.) Narrating Mobility, Boundaries and Belonging. Copenhagen: Centre for Development Research, Working Paper 99, 7, 49–64.

—— 2000. *Popular Culture, Gender Relations and the Democratization of Everyday Life in Kenya*, Journal of Southern African Studies 26 (2) 209–222.

—— 2002. *Mobile minds and socio-economic barriers: Livelihoods and African-American identifications among youth in Nairobi*. In N.N. Sørensen and K.F. Olwig (eds.) Work and Migration. Life and Livelihoods in a Globalizing World. London and New York: Routledge, 45–60.

Hake, A. 1977. *African Metropolis: Nairobi's Self-Help City*. London: Sussex University Press.

Hansen, K.T. 2005. *Space for Youth in Zambia's Patrimonial Politics? Draft of lecture presented at Centre for African Studies*, University of Copenhagen.

Jok, J.M. 2005. *War, Changing Ethics and the Position of Youth in South Sudan*. In J. Abbink and I. van Kessel (eds.) Vanguard or Vandals: Youth Politics and Conflict in Africa. Leiden, Boston: Brill Academic Publishers, 143–160.

Kaarsholm, P. 2006. *Violence as Signifier: Politics and Generational Struggle in KwaZulu-Natal*. P. Kaarsholm (ed.) Violence, Political Culture and Development in Africa. Oxford: James Currey, 139–160.

Kagwanja, P.M. 2005. *Clash of Generations? Youth Identity, violence and the politics of transition in Kenya, 1997-2202*. In J. Abbink and I. van Kessel (eds.) Vanguards or Vandals. Youth, Politics and Conflict in Africa. Leiden, Boston: Brill Academic Publishers, 81–109.

King, K. 1977. *The African Artisan*. London: Heinemann.

—— 1996. *Jua Kali Kenya: Change and Development in an Informal Economy*. London: James Currey.

McVicar, K. 1968. *Twilight of an African Slum. Pumwani and the Evolution of African Settlement in Nairobi*. Los Angeles CA: University of California.

Obbo, C. 1980. *African Women. Their Struggle for Economic Independence*. London: Zed Books.

O'Brien, D.B.C. 1996. *A Lost Generation? Youth Identity and State Decay in West Africa*. In R. Werbner and T.O. Ranger (eds.) Postcolonial Identities in Africa. London and New Jersey: Zed Books Ltd., 55–74.

Onduru, M.H.O. and F. Opondo 1996. *Pumwani Villages Population Census*. Nairobi.

Rashid, I. 1997. *Subaltern Reactions: Lumpen, Students and the Left*, Africa Development 22 (3/4) 19–45.

Richards, P. 1996. *Fighting for the Rain Forest: War, Youth and Resources in Sierra Leone*. Portsmouth NH: Heinemann.

Throup, D. 1987. *Economic and Social Origins of Mau Mau 1945-1953*. London: James Currey.

White, L. 1990. *The Comforts of Home: Prostitution in Colonial Nairobi*. Chicago IL: Chicago University Press.

Zlotnik, H. 1999. *Trends of International Migration Since 1965: What Existing Data Reveal*, International Migration 37 (1) 21–61.

AFRICAN MIGRATIONS: CONTINUITIES, DISCONTINUITIES
AND RECENT TRANSFORMATIONS

Oliver Bakewell and Hein de Haas

Introduction

Africa is often portrayed in both contemporary and historical accounts as a continent of people on the move (de Bruijn et al. 2001,
IOM 2005). Great migrations figure in the myths of origins for many
ethnic groups: for example, the Bantu expansion from central Africa,
the 'Hamitic myth' of migration from north to south, and even the
Voortrekkers 'Great Trek' in South Africa. While some of these migrations may be little more than hypotheses and lack any historical basis,
they all serve an important function in the (mythic) construction of
Africa and its people in the modern world (Bilger and Kraler 2005).
Today, new 'myths' about African migration are serving to shape
contemporary perceptions of Africa. For example, such modern myths
suggest that all Africans crossing the Sahara are in transit to Europe
or that the trafficking of women and children is the most common
form of migration within and from Nigeria.

The chronic lack of data about African migration has helped to
perpetuate such myths. The UN Population Division uses census data
to estimate the number of international migrants, but across Africa
such census data is often of poor quality or lacks any migration questions. As a result, 19 of the 56 countries in Africa have either no data
or just one census providing any information on migrant stock from
the 1950s (Zlotnik 2003: 3). Moreover, most of the border crossings
are over land frontiers that are passed with minimal if any formali-
ties. As a result there is only limited knowledge about the forms and
patterns of migration across large parts of Africa.

It is these movements *within* the continent that forms the vast
majority of African migration (Sander and Maimbo 2003). Although
there is some evidence that migration from Africa to industrialized
states is growing, it is important to recall that only a small fraction
of international migration originating in Africa results in journeys to
Europe, the Gulf, the US and beyond. As we will see, the conventional

focus on migration *out of* Africa conceals the existence of several migration sub-systems centred on continental migration poles such as Libya, Côte d'Ivoire, Ghana, Gabon and South Africa. Such a poor understanding of the nature and magnitude of intra-African migrations has skewed perceptions of migration within, from and towards the continent and allowed the development of these pervasive migration myths.

The aim of this chapter is to give a more balanced overview of migrations within and beyond the African continent. This is a risky and perhaps pretentious endeavour, given the huge size of the continent and the complexity and diversity of migrations found there. In the space available, we can only highlight some general migration trends and do not claim to offer a complete picture of African migrations. The following sections briefly summarize the evolution of migration patterns in different regions of Africa. Of course, these crude divisions between North, South, East and West are problematic, especially with reference to migration that cuts across such borders. Nevertheless, they will have to serve for the purpose of this broad overview. We conclude by outlining some of the recurring themes that are echoed across the continent and analyse the main research gaps.

North Africa and the Sahara

The pre-colonial population history of North Africa has been characterized by continually shifting patterns of human settlement. Nomadic or semi-nomadic (*transhumance*) groups traveled large distances with their herds between summer and winter pastures. Besides age-old patterns of circular migration, conquest and conflicts between tribal groups over natural resources and the control over trade routes were associated with the regular movement and resettlement of people. Throughout known history, there has been intensive population mobility between both sides of the Sahara through the trans-Saharan (caravan) trade, conquest, pilgrimage, and religious education. The Sahara itself is a huge transition zone, and the diverse ethnic composition of Saharan oases testifies to this long history of population mobility.

In all north-African countries, colonial intrusion occurring as of the mid nineteenth century has triggered processes of urbanization, settlement by *colons* (colonialists) and substantial rural-to-urban migration. However, colonialism was only associated with substantial international movement in the 'French' Maghreb. From the second half of the nineteenth century, Tunisian and Moroccan workers moved to 'French' Algeria to work. During the First and Second World Wars, a lack of labor power in France led to the recruitment of Maghrebi factory and mine workers as well as soldiers. After Morocco and Tunisia became independent in 1956 this 'colonial' migration to France largely persisted (de Haas 2007). After independence in 1962, over one million *colons* and *harkis* (Algerians who served with the French army in the war of independence) left Algeria.

Post-colonial labor migration to France was modest compared with the 1963–1972 migration boom. Rapid post-war economic growth in northwest Europe and increasing unskilled labor shortages and labor recruitment by France, Germany, Belgium and the Netherlands triggered large-scale emigration of "guest workers" from Morocco and Tunisia. While Tunisia and Morocco pursued pro-emigration policies, and Algeria's stance towards emigration to France was more ambivalent, the Egyptian state actively discouraged labor emigration in the 1960s (Choucri 1977, Sell 1988).

The shock of the 1973 Oil Crisis and the ensuing economic recession in Western Europe would dramatically reshape the North African migration landscape. For Maghrebi-European migration, it heralded the end of the 'recruitment phase' and the onset of increasingly restrictive immigration policies pursued by European states. For the Arab oil countries the events of 1973 marked the *beginning* of massive labor recruitment. Coinciding with the implementation of Sadat's *infitah* ('open door') policies, this facilitated large-scale migration of unskilled and skilled laborers from Egypt. Smaller but substantial numbers of migrants came from Sudan, the Maghreb countries and the Horn of Africa. The oil crisis also created the condition for the emergence of a new migration pole *within* North Africa. Rapidly increasing oil revenues and economic growth in oil-rich Libya triggered substantial movement of mostly temporary migrants, mainly from Egypt, but also from Sudan and other Maghreb countries (Hamood 2006).

Economic downturn and mass unemployment in Europe provided the mirror image of the boom of the Arab oil economies. Nevertheless, large number of Maghrebi migrants ended up staying permanently, while subsequent family and irregular migration explain the continuous increase of Maghrebi emigrant populations throughout the 1980s and 1990s (Entzinger 1985, Fargues 2004). Furthermore, after 1990 there has been a striking resumption of labor migration of Maghrebis but now also Egyptians to southern Europe. Particularly in Italy and Spain, economic growth has generated increasing demand for flexible and low-skilled labor (Fargues 2004: 1357). An increasing proportion of such independent labor migrants in Europe are women (cf. Salih 2001). In Algeria, the outbreak of the civil war in 1991 led to an increase of refugee and economic migration to an increasingly diverse array of European countries (Collyer 2003). Although many immigrants are irregular, southern European governments have been compelled to grant legal status to large numbers of migrants on several occasions since the late 1980s. Another development has been the increasing migration of higher educated Maghrebis to Canada (Québec) and the US (Fargues 2005).

Meanwhile, in the Gulf, economic stagnation due to falling oil prices from 1983 and increasing reliance on Asian immigrant labor caused a decline in demand for Arab workers (Zohry and Harrell-Bond 2003: 27–31). The 1991 Gulf War led to massive expulsions (Baldwin-Edwards 2005: 28). Nevertheless, African migration to the Gulf has often been more persistent and permanent than the *temporary* migration policies intended. In fact, after the Gulf war, migration rates quickly resumed to pre-War levels (Zohry and Harrell-Bond 2003: 30, 35). Semi-legal migrants enter through intricate systems of visa-trading (IOM 2005: 60), and undocumented labor migrants enter the Gulf through making the *hadj*, the Muslim pilgrimage to Mecca.

Although the advent of colonialism had caused a decline in traditional trans-Saharan mobility, soon after independence the foundations were laid for contemporary trans-Saharan migration. In the 1970s and 1980s, forced and voluntary settlement of nomads and wars in the Sahel zone provoked two types of Saharan mobility. First, (former) nomads and traders, such as the Touareg, started migrating to work at construction sites and the oil fields of southern Algeria and Libya. Second, with recurrent warfare in the entire Sahel zone, thousands of refugees settled in towns and cities in Libya, Algeria, Mauritania, and Egypt (Bredeloup and Pliez 2005).

Libya's pan-African policies of the 1990s would cause a major increase in trans-Saharan migration. Disappointed by the perceived lack of support from fellow Arab countries during the air and arms embargo imposed on Libya by the UN Security Council between 1992 and 2000, Colonel Al-Qadhafi positioned himself as an African leader and started to encourage sub-Saharan Africans to work in Libya in the spirit of pan-African solidarity (Hamood 2006). In the early 1990s, most migrants came from Libya's neighbours Sudan, Chad and Niger, which subsequently developed into transit countries for migrants from a much wider array of sub-Saharan countries (Bredeloup and Pliez 2005: 6). In the same period, violence, civil wars and economic decline affecting in several parts of West Africa (Sierra Leone, Liberia, Côte d'Ivoire and Nigeria), Central Africa (Democratic Republic of Congo), East Africa (Sudan) and the Horn of Africa (Somalia, Eritrea) also contributed to increasing trans-Saharan migration (de Haas 2006a).

Since 1995, this mixed group of sub-Saharan asylum seekers and labor migrants have gradually joined Maghrebis who illegally cross the Strait of Gibraltar to Spain or from Tunisia to Italy (Barros et al. 2002, Boubakri 2004: 3). This has been further incited by increasing xenophobia and expulsions in Libya after violent anti-immigrant riots occurred in 2000 (Hamood 2006). Increased border controls have led to a general diversification in attempted crossing points (Boubakri 2004: 5, de Haas 2006a) from the eastern Moroccan coast to Algeria, from Tunisia's coast to Libya, and from the Western Sahara and most recently Mauritania and other West-African countries to the Canary Islands. A substantial proportion of migrants consider North Africa (in particular Libya) as their primary destination, whereas others failing or not venturing to enter Europe prefer to stay in north-Africa as a "second best option" rather than return to their more unstable and substantially poorer origin countries (Barros et al. 2002, Bredeloup and Pliez 2005).

Approximately 4.7 and 2.4 million north African migrants and their descendants were believed to live in Europe and Arab countries, respectively, around 2004 (Fargues 2005). Morocco has the largest officially registered emigrant population of all countries involved with 3.1 million expatriates including second generation descendants, followed by Egypt (2.7 million), Algeria (1.4 million) and Tunisia (840,000). According to various estimates, at least 100,000 sub-Saharan migrants now live in both Mauritania and Algeria, 1 to 1.5 million in Libya, and anywhere between 2.2 and 4 million mainly Sudanese in Egypt. Tunisia and Morocco house smaller but growing sub-Saharan immigrant communities of several tens of thousands (de Haas 2006a).

East Africa and the Horn of Africa

The migration patterns of this region have been dominated by circular movement of various forms for many generations, especially among the large numbers of pastoralists. Moving with their livestock to grazing land and forage has involved both seasonal migration within stable patterns, and population drift as the orbit of people's migrations shifts with the changing ecological, political and economic environment. Such free ranging movement across the region has come under steady pressure for over a century as the imposition of colonial rule, the creation of borders, sedentary development initiatives and violent conflict have all contributed to constrain the range of pastoralism.

Like the rest of the continent, migration patterns across East Africa and the Horn were profoundly altered by the arrival of European colonialists and their attempts to marshal the labor of Africans to serve their interests. The arrival of European settlers forced Africans off their land, especially in the Kenyan highlands, which were the focus of European settlement in the region. Colonial policies coerced people to engage in the cash economy by undertaking wage labor on settler farms and estates; working on coffee and cocoa plantations in Uganda and providing labor for the mines of the Belgian Congo. Although this represented a major expansion of labor migration, the practice was already established. For example, areas which had been supplying porters for the caravans crossing the region through the nineteenth century, provided the majority of the laborers in the German plantations of East Africa (Iliffe 1995: 207). There has also been a high level of migration from rural areas to the emerging urban centres, such as Nairobi and Dar es Salaam, but the extent of urbanization in this region has remained lower than other parts of the continent.

During the colonial period, the British allowed labor migrants to move freely between Kenya, Uganda and Tanzania and this was continued with independence with the establishment of the East African Community (EAC). This freedom of movement ended in 1977 when the EAC collapsed (IOM 2000). The EAC was revived in 1999 with a treaty which committed member states to facilitate the freedom of movement for their citizens within the community. The creation of the East African Passport was one of its first concrete steps.

The region has the dubious distinction of both generating and hosting over 50% of the refugees on the continent. In the last forty years, since the end of colonialism large swathes of East Africa and the Horn has been scarred by long and pervasive conflicts; only Kenya and Tanzania have been spared war or civil conflict. As a result, there have been massive movements of refugees exchanged between the countries of the region—for example, Ethiopians in Sudan, Sudanese

Table 1. Refugees in East Africa and the Horn 1995–2005

	1995	2000	2005
Burundi	142,700	27,136	20,681
Djibouti	25,700	23,243	10,456
Eritrea	1,100	1,984	4,418
Ethiopia	393,500	197,959	100,817
Kenya	239,500	206,106	251,271
Rwanda	7,800	28,398	45,206
Somalia	600	558	493
Sudan	558,200	414,928	147,256
Tanzania	829,700	680,862	548,824
Uganda	229,300	236,622	257,256
Total	2,428,100	1,817,796	1,386,678

Source: UNHCR (http://www.unhcr.org/statistics.html).

in Ethiopia—and beyond, especially to Egypt and DR Congo. Many refugees in the region have been pushed back and forth across borders in 'search of cool ground' as violence has waxed and waned (Allen and Turton 1996) or forced to flee to a third country as their country of first asylum has been overtaken by conflict.

Until 1996, the policy of East African state towards refugees was generally accommodating, despite the ongoing complaints about the lack of resources and the failure of 'burden sharing' with industrialized states (Stein 1987). The expulsion of Rwandan refugees by Tanzania in 1996 signalled the end of the international community's easy reliance on notions of 'African hospitality' as a rationale for African states to accept refugees. Since then climate for refugees has worsened; states are becoming more reluctant to grant asylum and more enthusiastic to hasten repatriation (Betts and Milner 2006: 24). Consequently, there has been a very significant decrease in the number of refugees in the region (see table 1).

However, there has been no commensurate decline in violent conflict and more people than ever are being forced from their homes. Today, the vast majority of these forced migrants are unable to cross international borders. At the end of 2005, there were estimated to be over 5 million 'internally displaced persons' in Sudan alone, with a further 1.7 million in Uganda (USCRI 2006).

Perhaps not surprisingly, the overwhelming focus of migration research and policy in East Africa and the Horn has been on forced migration. Little is known about the scale of other forms of international migration in the region but the available estimates suggest that they represent the majority of cross-border movements. According to the UN Population Division, the number of international migrants living in the region has declined from a peak of nearly 5 million in 1990 to 3.4 million by 2005 (UN 2006). Much of this decline is related to the reduction in the number of refugees. Given the porous nature of the borders, the lack of controls, the very limited census data and problems of access in conflict zones, these estimates almost certainly understate the movement of people. In countries such as Somalia and Sudan that are caught up in conflict where migrants are often granted *prima facie*[1] refugee status, attempting to distinguish 'forced' from 'voluntary' migration is unlikely to be possible or useful. It is likely that much of the seasonal and labor migration in the region is now caught up in the broad category of forced migration.

There are significant levels of migration out of the region, most notably to the Gulf, South Africa, Europe and the United States. The effect of the 'brain drain' has been a major concern in the region for many years. Uganda experienced a massive loss of its educated and skilled people during the 1970s during the rule of Amin, in particular with the expulsion of Ugandan Asians. This benefited both countries that received them including Uganda's neighbours, Kenya and Tanzania (Black et al. 2004a), and Britain. Ethiopia has lost large numbers of graduates who have not returned after study abroad. In 2003 Ethiopians were the second largest group of immigrants to the US and they have been in the top four countries since at least 1990. Refugees from Sudan, Somalia and Ethiopia are among the largest groups accepted for resettlement in the US (a combined total of 6,000 in 2003) (US DHS 2004). There are also irregular movements of migrants to Europe from East Africa and the Horn to Europe, especially Somalis, Eritreans and Sudanese. The levels of migration from the region to South Africa and Libya as well as labor migration from the Horn to the Gulf are thought to be significant but there are few reliable data available on these movements (Black et al. 2004a).

---

[1] I.e. a person is granted refugee status by virtue of having come from a country rather than by going through an individual refugee status determination procedure (Hyndman and Nylund 1998).

West Africa

Contemporary West Africa has recently often been described as the most "mobile" part of Africa. According to census data, West Africa houses the largest international migrant population, amounting to 6.8 million in 2000, or 2.7 percent of its total population (Zlotnik 2004). However, this figure fails to capture migration to other parts of Africa, Europe, North America and the Gulf, which is also higher than elsewhere, with the exception of North Africa.

As in other parts of Africa, there is evidence of a considerable degree of pre-colonial mobility, which is for instance testified by the dispersion of Fulani speaking people through large parts of the Sahel zone and the seasonal wanderings of transhumant herders (cf. Arthur 1991). Furthermore, trans-Saharan trade, religious education and the *hadj* to Mecca was associated with major mobility and sometimes settlement of West Africans all across West, North and East Africa.

Colonization would affect most of these patterns. When the first Europeans arrived in the 15th century, they disrupted traditional patterns of (trans-Saharan) trade and seasonal movement while the growing slave trade led to the transportation of an approximate 12 million Africans across the Atlantic (Anarfi and Kwankye 2003, Bump 2006). Since the late nineteenth century, colonization and the establishment of cocoa, coffee and groundnut plantations, infrastructure works and the growth of cities such as Accra, Lagos, Kano, Ibadan, Abidjan, Lomé, Dakar and Cotonou triggered major rural-rural and rural-urban migration (Arthur 1991). Other factors that are believed to have stimulated such migration were infrastructure improvements, the introduction of colonial taxes (Arthur 1991), organized labor recruitment (Bump 2006), and the expropriation of agricultural land for plantations (Amin 1974).

Intra-regional mobility in West Africa is generally characterized by a predominantly North-South, inland-coast movement from Sahel West Africa (Mali, Burkina Faso, Niger and Chad) to the plantations, mines and cities of coastal West Africa (predominantly Côte d'Ivoire, Liberia, Ghana, Nigeria, and in the West to Senegal and The Gambia) (Findley 2004, Arthur 1991, Kress 2006). Most intra-regional migration is seasonal or circular, reflecting pre-colonial patterns, although many migrants have eventually settled. After independence in the late 1950s and 1960s, the relatively prosperous economies of Ghana and Côte d'Ivoire attracted large numbers of internal and international migrants from countries such as Togo and Nigeria (mainly to Ghana), Burkina Faso and Guinea (mainly to Côte d'Ivoire) and Niger and Mali (to both). In a strong anti-colonial spirit of pan-Africanism, the governments of Ghana and particularly Côte d'Ivoire welcomed immigrants to work and stay (cf. Anarfi and Kwankye 2003).

Increasing repression in Ghana following the 1966 coup, a declining economy and rising unemployment marked the country's transition to an emigration country. The immigrant community in Ghana became a scapegoat for the deteriorating situation and in 1969 the Ghanaian government enacted the Aliens Compliance Order, leading to a mass expulsion of an estimated 155,000 to 213,000 migrants, predominantly from Nigeria, working informally in the cocoa industry. Ghanaians also started emigrating in large numbers. An estimated two million Ghanaian workers left Ghana between 1974 and 1981; their primary destinations being Nigeria and Côte d'Ivoire. Also skilled Ghanaians such as teachers, doctors and administrators moved to Nigeria, Uganda, Botswana, and Zambia. As of the mid 1980s, Ghanaians have increasingly migrated to a range of destinations in Europe and North America (Anarfi and Kwankye 2003, Bump 2006).

While migration to Côte d'Ivoire continued, Nigeria took over Ghana's place as West Africa's second migration pole after the 1973 Oil Crisis. Similar to Libya and the Gulf countries, the surge in oil prices made oil-rich Nigeria into a major African migration destination. However, misguided economic policies and a major decline in oil production and prices heralded a long period of economic downturn accompanied by sustained political repression. In 1983 and 1985, Nigeria followed the Ghanaian example and expelled an estimated two million low skilled west-African migrants, including over one million Ghanaians (Bump 2006, Arthur 1991: 74). As Ghana had before, Nigeria transformed itself from a net immigration to a net emigration country (Black et al. 2004b: 11), although many immigrants (in particular Beninois and Ghanaians) have remained.

Meanwhile, the formation of the Economic Community of West African States (ECOWAS) in 1975 expanded migration opportunities for West Africans. The freedom of mobility is enshrined in the ECOWAS protocol of 29 May 1979 on the Free Movement of Persons, the Right of Residence and Establishment. However, the implementation of the protocol leaves much to be desired (Adepoju 2001), as is testified by past expulsions and by police and border officials taking bribes as forms of unofficial toll (de Haas 2006b).

The general worsening of the political and economic situation in West Africa over the 1980s set the stage for a change in the West African migration landscape. This trend was reinforced by civil wars in Sierra Leone (1991–2001), Liberia (1989–1996 and 1999–2003), Guinea (1999–2000) and Côte d'Ivoire since 2002, leading to the loss of up to a quarter-million lives and at least 1.1 million people living as refugees or internally displaced persons (Drumtra 2003). After 1993, political turmoil, economic decline and rising nationalism in Côte d'Ivoire, West Africa's only remaining labor migration pole with an approximate quarter of its population consisting of immigrants, prompted hundreds of thousands of migrants, predominantly Burkinabè but also Malians, to flee the country (Black et al. 2004b, Drumtra 2003, Findley 2004, Kress 2006).

Although many settled migrants would stay (cf. Adepoju 2000) and other returned, the civil wars and particularly the crisis in Côte d'Ivoire fundamentally affected West African migration patterns. Confronted with the lack of alternative migration destinations in the region, skilled and low skilled West Africans expanded their geographical view culminating into a diversification of destinations (Bump 2006). This coincided with the emergence of two new migration poles at the northern and southern extremes of the continent over the 1990s, that is, 'pan-African' Libya and post-apartheid South Africa (Adepoju 2004, Bredeloup and Pliez 2005). Also Gabon and Botswana have emerged as new destinations (Adepoju 2000). Due to increasing trans-Saharan migration to Libya, other Maghreb countries and the EU, Mauritania, Senegal, Mali, Nigeria, Niger and Chad have developed into transit countries (de Haas 2006a).

Until 1980, only limited numbers of West African students and workers migrated to industrialized countries, mainly following the French-English colonial divide. In comparison to North Africa, extra-continental migration remained very limited. Only workers from Cape Verde (to Portugal and the Netherlands) and parts of the Senegal river basin in northern Senegal and western Mali (to France) joined the northbound, large-scale movement of north-African labor migrants of the 1960s and 1970s (Carling 2001, Findley 2004).

Since the late 1980s, however, there has been a remarkable increase and diversification of migration to Europe and North America, principally from Nigeria, Ghana and Senegal. This has comprised both highly skilled migration, for instance of health workers to the UK, the US and the Gulf, and relatively low skilled, often irregular, migration, in particular to the informal economies of Libya and (mainly southern) Europe. Irregular emigrants tend to work in informal services, construction and agriculture, while more and more emigrants are self-employed entrepreneurs (Adepoju 2000). Increasing immigration restrictions in Europe have not led to a decrease in emigration but rather its increasingly irregular character and growing costs. This has made migrants more vulnerable to exploitation and trafficking. In particular trafficking of young women who work in prostitution in Europe is a subject of major policy concern (Carling 2006).

According to official figures, 351,000 West Africans are living in the US, 41,000 in Canada, 288,000 in France, 176,000 in the UK, 82,000 in Italy, and 68,000 in Portugal (OECD 2006). In the US, the dominant origin countries of West Africans are Nigeria (135,000), Ghana (66,000) and Liberia (39,000) (Dixon 2006). In the EU, Nigeria, Senegal, Ghana, Cape Verde, Mali and Côte d'Ivoire provide the largest numbers of migrants from the region. In recent years, migration to Italy, Spain and Portugal and the US has particularly increased (Black et al. 2004b).

Southern Africa

For many of the peoples of southern Africa, the story of their origins is one of migrations: in response to conquest; in search of new land; or to resolve power struggles. For example, many of the peoples of Zambia and eastern Angola see their origins in the upper Kasai, DR Congo, and recount the journeys which brought their ancestors into new lands (von Oppen 1995, White 1960). Moreover, individuals, households and whole villages continued to move within rural areas, causing dismay to colonial officials (Ferguson 1999: 39). In such contexts,

> migration—rather than being a disruption to normal household life and composition—constitutes the very form of households. Movement of people between households (residential units) is the norm rather than the exception (de Haan 2000: 20–21).

As European influence spread in from the coasts, it stimulated new forms of mobility. The Portuguese first came to Angola in the 15th century but it was only in the 18th century that they started to move inland in search of slaves (Miller 1988). Some chiefs cooperated with the trade and moved to the east in search of captives, forcing others to flee. In the nineteenth century, with the end of the Atlantic slave trade, the search turned to rubber, ivory and later beeswax, which encouraged more Africans to move deeper into the forests of the interior.

With the arrival of European settlers and the establishment of the mines of South Africa and the Zambian Copperbelt, especially after the discovery of gold in the Witwatersrand, more sophisticated systems to control African labor were devised. Initially migrants came independently but were subject to increasing regulation in an attempt to prevent them settling permanently and maintain the circular flow of people. While the migrant labor system stretched over the region to serve the mines and farms of Zimbabwe, Namibia, Zambia, Swaziland and Botswana, its core has always been in South Africa. By 1920 there were 100,000 foreign contract laborers working in South African mines from all over the region. At its peak in 1970, this had risen to 265,000 and declined to 192,000 in 1990 (Crush 2005).

The formal system of labor migration for the mines was supplemented by a parallel system of irregular migration that provided labor for other sectors, including farms and plantations, domestic services, transport and construction. In 1951, South African census data recorded over 600,000 foreign born Africans in South Africa. This declined steadily with the increasing grip of apartheid, but even in 1985 there were over 300,000 (ibid.). The contract labor system was heavily biased towards men and the movement of women was mostly restricted to irregular channels. As a result the extent of women's migration has remained largely unrecorded.

Despite the attempts to avoid permanent settlement around the mines, the industrial development stimulated the growth of urban areas, driven by both internal rural-urban migration and international migration. With the growth of the Copperbelt, Zambia became one of the most urbanized countries in Africa with 40% of the population living in urban areas (according to the 1990 census). With the end of apartheid, South Africa has experienced a rapid rise in internal migration as people who were previously forced to stay in rural areas have been free to move to the cities (ibid.: 16).

Many commentators have described the southern African migration system (both formal and informal) as a means to exploit the African labor to serve the interests of capitalism, especially as developed under apartheid (Burawoy 1976, Meillassoux 1983, Wolpe 1972). While there is little doubt that this is the case, the analysis often leads to the portrayal of the African migrants as passive pawns of wider forces and the system as destroying a largely sedentary 'traditional' life. However, where these coercive systems have broken down or never even existed, migration from rural areas to the cities continues unabated (Peil and Sada 1984). The single explanatory factor in determining migration, the logic of capitalism, does not cast much light on the reasons for some people staying at home and others going; nor do they explain the different responses to migration pressures in different villages. The assumption of coercion does not account for the widespread practice of migration before colonialization nor the willing co-operation of black Africans in providing labor for capitalist enterprizes (Peil and Sada 1984, Wright 1995).

In the second half of the twentieth century, the region was embroiled in some of the most entrenched conflicts on the continent. The liberation wars in Mozambique, Angola, Zimbabwe and Namibia and the struggle against the apartheid regime in South Africa displaced thousands of people within the region. The front line states of Zambia, Malawi, and Zimbabwe (after independence in 1980) hosted the majority of refugees. By the late 1980s, the one million Mozambican refugees in Malawi represented nearly one in ten of the population (Russell et al. 1990). With the repatriation of Mozambican refugees, Zambia became the leading country of asylum in the region, with over 200,000 Angolan refugees and 60,000 Congolese in 2001. Since the end of the war in 2002, many Angolan refugees have repatriated from Zambia. However, there are estimated to be over a one million people internally displaced within Angola and movement within the country is heavily constrained by the lack of infrastructure and the prevalence of landmines.[2] In the last five years, the collapse of Zimbabwe has generated new internal displacement and refugees in the region.

Since 1990, the context for migration in southern Africa has been transformed. The end of the wars in Namibia, Mozambique and eventually Angola, and the defeat of apartheid in South Africa have heralded a new set of migration motivations and opportunities in the region. Refugees and exiles have been returning to their countries and thousands of others have seized the chance to move. The attitudes to migration among the countries of the region have become increas-

---

[2] Figures according to UNHCR (http://www.unhcr.org).

ingly negative with more controls on immigration and restrictions on migrants' rights. Rather than reducing migration, the result has been to drive it underground and there has been a significant growth in the numbers of undocumented migrants. In particular, South Africa has become a focus for migration both from within the region and the rest of Africa. Estimates of the numbers of migrants in South Africa vary wildly ranging down from the wildly exaggerated figure of eight to ten million to the more plausible total of half to one million (Crush 2005: 12, Kihato and Landau 2006, Landau 2004).

Emigration from the region has also become a topic of increasing concern, especially with the departure of large numbers of people with high levels of education and skills. Since independence, the poorer countries of the region such as Malawi and Zambia have struggled to retain professional staff in public services, most notably in the face of recruitment drives to attract nurses and doctors into the UK health service. Since the end of apartheid and South Africa's re-engagement with the rest of the world, the so-called brain drain has grown as more skilled South Africans have emigrated to industrialized states. At the same time, South Africa has also generated a regional brain drain as it has attracted skilled migrants from its neighbouring countries. Despite the level of concern, there are very limited data available to assess the scale of the brain drain in the region (see Crush 2005, McDonald and Crush 2002).

There have been various attempts to harmonize migration policies across the region but these have been unsuccessful to date. The Southern African Development Community attempted to introduce a protocol on the freedom of movement but this was opposed most vigorously by South Africa, Botswana and Namibia. A weaker protocol on the facilitation of movement has now been adopted in 2005 but has yet to be signed by sufficient member states to come into effect (Williams and Carr 2006).

Conclusion

This brief overview illustrates the diversity of migration patterns across the African continent. However, there are certain recurrent themes that are echoed across the different regions reflecting their linkages and shared experiences.

First, in all regions, it is clear that colonialism has had a profound impact on migration in Africa. The direct intervention of European powers to control African labor through slavery, expropriation of land and contract labor systems both forced and encouraged new movements. The establishment of new industrial centres and urban areas set in train the rural-urban migration, which became a major pre-occupation for colonial and independent African governments. President Nyerere's policy of villagization in Tanzania in the late 1960s set a pattern of development interventions in rural areas all across the continent to reduce the levels of out-migration to the urban areas that continues to this day. For example, in 2003 the African Development Bank gave loans and grants to the value of $86 million to Ethiopia to support rural infrastructure and financial services to 'tackle migration' to urban areas from rural communities (Black et al. 2004, IRIN 2003). Despite such efforts, the levels of urbanization have increased across Africa.

The other critical legacy of colonial powers on African migration was the imposition of borders, which laid the foundations for the modern nation states. While the borders represented an attempt by colonial authorities to control the movement of people and extract their labor or taxes, at the same time they defined the extent of their authority. For those near the borders, rather than fleeing long distances to escape taxation, forced labor or other such impositions, it was merely necessary for them to cross a line. By judicious crossing of frontiers, it was (and to a certain extent still is) possible to get the best, or at least avoid the worst, of both worlds (Nugent 1996). Hence, while the borders did control some migration, they created new forms of migration by reshaping 'political and economic opportunity structures' (Tornimbeni 2005). This is seen most clearly in the case of refugees, who can only gain international recognition and protection if they leave their country of origin.

The arbitrary nature of the borders means that distinction between international and internal migration is somewhat muddied in the African setting. In many cases, a move to a neighbouring country may involve less social and political upheaval for the migrant than a move to the capital (Adepoju 1995). The weak control of the state in many countries, especially on their remote borders, may also mean the change in jurisdiction does not influence migrant behaviour as it might in other contexts.

Second, there are many threads of continuity linking pre-colonial, colonial and post-colonial migration patterns. While colonization, war and major political-economic shocks such as the 1973 Oil Crisis clearly created major shifts in migration patterns, they were overlaid on existing migration practices and patterns rather working on a *tabula rasa*. As the context changes, the old patterns can show through more strongly again: for example, an increasing number of contemporary migrants from sub-Saharan Africa are using ancient Saharan caravan trading and migration routes on their journey to North Africa. Indeed in the case of the southern African labor migration system, its success depended on the widespread practice of migration prior to colonization that encouraged the movement of Africans. It is particularly important to recognize the *continuity* between current migration paths and those of the past, because this is the only way to identify areas of *discontinuity* and their structural causes.

Across the continent, the 'brain drain' is a recurrent concern among African governments. It is true that African migrants to Europe and the US have the highest levels of education among all migrants, although the US attracts more highly skilled migrants than Europe (Katseli et al. 2006, Schmidley 2001). Emigration of skilled workers is said to have created labor shortages in specific sectors, such as among health care workers in Ghana and South Africa. On the other hand, the prevalence of mass unemployment among highly educated people in Africa casts some doubt on the assumption that emigration would automatically represent a loss. In fact, there is very limited data available to assess the true scale and effects of the brain drain.

In contrast to popular belief, there has not been a recent 'major increase' in intra-African migrations. West Africa is the only part of Africa where migration populations relative to the total population have been increasing over the past decades, while other parts of Africa have shown a relative and sometimes even *absolute* decline (Zlotnik 2004). Only North Africa has relatively high levels of extra-continental migration. Even in West Africa, where migration to the industrialized countries is higher than elsewhere south of the Sahara, regional migration still is at least seven times higher than migration from West Africa to the rest of the world (OECD 2006).

Recent changes in African migration patterns have been affected by the rise (e.g., South Africa, Libya, Gabon, Botswana) and fall (e.g., Ghana, Nigeria, Côte d'Ivoire) of migration poles on the continent, as well as civil wars affecting several parts of West Africa, Sudan, the Horn of Africa and the Great Lakes region. There seems to be increasing inter-linkages between the migration sub-systems centred around these continental migration poles as well as migration systems that link Africa to Europe, the Gulf and North America. This has coincided with a recent *diversification* of intra-continental migration patterns and a significant, albeit modest, increase in migration *out of* Africa. While the absolute numbers of African migrants to Europe might be increasing, they are falling as a percentage of overall immigration level (Katseli et al. 2006). The picture in the US is very different. In 2005, only 3% of the foreign born population had been born in Africa. However, this represents an increase from 1% in 1995 and a four fold increase in absolute numbers up from 270,000 in 1995 to 1.1 million in 2005.[3]

Finally, across all the regions and over many decades, there have been laments about the lack of data and the limited research into migration in Africa. In some ways, this must echo the problems found in other fields in a continent where resources are extremely limited. There seemed to be more consistent and reliable migration research in the 1970s. However as African economies declined, many countries suffered the ravages of war and migration dropped off the policy agenda, the interest in migration waned. Today, the trends in research seem to clearly follow the concerns of policy rather than any academic agenda. Unfortunately, migration research, which requires consistent effort over a sustained period, has been subject to the vagaries of short term funding focused on 'hot topics'. Hence, in East Africa, we no longer hear about labor migration but most current research and literature is focused on forced migration. Likewise, in West Africa we hear more about trafficking; and in North Africa about migration to Europe. While all these aspects of migration are of great importance, by focusing on these areas under the policy spotlight, we fail to see the underlying trends in mobility across the continent, which affect the lives of millions more people.

What is distinctive about much of the current literature on African migration is its portrayal of African migrants as subject to external

---

[3] Figures according to the Migration Information Source Global Data Center (http://www.migrationinformation.org/Global/Data/).

forces that drive their movements. This is seen most clearly in the structuralist literature, which shows how Africa migration patterns have been shaped by the interests of capital and states. For example, Amin suggests that the endeavour to understand migration through the analysis of individual's motivations is futile since the migrant 'rationalizes the objective needs of his situation' (Amin 1974). Modern discourses of migration in Africa tend to present it as either: a desperate move to escape poverty; forced migration by those subject to violence or the threat of violence; trafficking and smuggling; or, migration in response to global forces and environmental misfortune.

This completely ignores the insights from the contemporary migration literature that highlight the ambivalent and complex relationships between poverty and migration. What is desperately missing is any understanding of the agency of African migrants in the process of movement, even in the face of enormous constraints. There is little recognition of 'the importance of social practices emerging from below in shaping migration practices' (Andersson 2006: 377). This portrayal of African migrants as subject to forces completely beyond their control appears to be a reflection of the common 'image of Africa as a continent in the grip of powerful external forces, with most of what happens in countries being fairly directly attributable to external factors' (Booth 2003: 868), rather than a conclusion drawn from empirical evidence.

It is important to stress that by highlighting such themes we are not trying to suggest that there is an essentially 'African' form of migration, which can be analytically distinguished from that found in the rest of the world. Too much of the literature of Africa suggests it is an 'exception', thereby cutting it off from the mainstream of theory and debate (Bilger and Kraler 2005: 6, Roe 1995). Instead, we would argue that understanding the dynamics of migration in the context of Africa is necessary in order to understand the human experience of mobility.

References

Adepoju, A. 1995. *Migration in Africa*. In J. Baker and T.A. Aina (eds.) The Migration Experience in Africa. Uppsala: Nordika Afrikainstitutet, 87–108.
—— 2000. *Issues and Recent Trends in International Migration in Sub-Saharan Africa*, International Social Science Journal (165) 383–394.

—— 2001. *Regional Organisations and Intra-Regional Migration in Sub-Saharan Africa: Challenges and Prospects*, International Migration 39 (6) 43–59.

—— 2004. *Changing Configurations of Migration in Africa*. Migration Information Source (http://www.migrationinformation.org/Feature/display.cfm?ID=251) (accessed 9 January 2007).

Alioua, M. 2005. *La migration transnationale des Africains subsahariens au Maghreb: L'exemple de l'étape marocaine*, Maghreb Machrek (185) 37–57.

Allen, T. and D. Turton 1996. *Introduction: in search of cool ground*. In T. Allen (ed.) In Search of Cool Ground: War, Flight and Homecoming in Northeast Africa. London: James Currey, 1–22.

Amin, S. (ed.) 1974. *Modern Migrations in Western Africa*. London: Oxford University Press.

Anarfi, J. and S. Kwankye 2003. *Migration from and to Ghana: A Background Paper*. University of Sussex: DRC on Migration, Globalisation and Poverty (Working Paper; C4).

Andersson, J.A. 2006. *Informal Moves, Informal Markets: International Migrants and Traders from Mzimba District*, Malawi, African Affairs 105 (420) 375–397.

Arthur, J.A. 1991. *International Labor Migration Patterns in West Africa*, African Studies Review 34 (3) 65–87.

Baldwin-Edwards, M. 2005. *Migration in the Middle East and Mediterranean*. Greece: Mediterranean Migration Observatory.

Barros, L., M. Lahlou, C. Escoffier, P. Pumares and P. Ruspini 2002. *L'immigration Irrégulière Subsaharienne à Travers et Vers le Maroc*. Geneva: International Labour Organisation.

Betts, A. and J. Milner 2006. *The Externalisation of EU Asylum Policy: The Position of African States*. Oxford: University of Oxford, Centre on Migration, Policy and Society (COMPAS Working Papers).

Bilger, V. and A. Kraler 2005. *Introduction: African migrations. Historical perspectives and contemporary dynamics*, Wiener Zeitschrift für kritische Afrikastudien; Special Issue—African Migrations. Historical Perspectives and Contemporary Dynamics (8) 5–21.

Black, R., L.M. Hilker and C. Pooley 2004a. *Migration and Pro-Poor Policy in East Africa*. Sussex: University of Sussex, Development Research Centre on Migration, Globalisation and Poverty.

Black, R., S. Ammassari, S. Mouillesseaux and R. Rajkotia 2004b. *Migration and Pro-Poor Policy in West Africa*. Sussex: University of Sussex, Development Research Centre on Migration, Globalisation and Poverty (Working Paper C8).

Booth, D. 2003. *Patterns of Difference and Practical Theory: Researching the New Poverty Strategy Processes in Africa*, Journal of International Development 15 (7) 863–877.

Boubakri, H. 2004. *Transit migration between Tunisia, Libya and Sub-Saharan Africa: study based on Greater Tunis*. Paper presented at the Regional Conference on 'Migrants in transit countries: sharing responsibility for management and protection', Istanbul, 30 September–1 October 2004. Strasbourg: Council of Europe.

Bredeloup, S. and O. Pliez 2005. *Editorial: Migrations entre les deux rives du Sahara*, Autrepart 4 (36) 3–20.

Bump, M. 2006. *Ghana: Searching for Opportunities at Home and Abroad*, Migration Information Source (http://www.migrationinformation.org), March.

Burawoy, M. 1976. *The Functions and Reproduction of Migrant Labour: Comparative Material from Southern Africa and the United States*, American Journal of Sociology 81 (5) 1050–1087.

Carling, J. 2001. *Aspiration and ability in international migration: Cape Verdean experiences of mobility and immobility*. Dissertations & Theses, 2001/5. Centre for Development and the Environment, University of Oslo.

—— 2006. Migration, *Human Smuggling and Trafficking from Nigeria to Europe*. Geneva: International Organisation for Migration.

Choucri, N. 1977. *The New Migration in the Middle East: A Problem for Whom?*, International Migration Review 11 (4) 412–443.

Collyer, M. 2003. *Explaining Change in Established Migration Systems: The Movement of Algerians to France and the UK.* Sussex: University of Sussex, Sussex Centre for Migration Research (Migration Working Paper; 16).

Crush, J. 2005. *Migration in Southern Africa.* Geneva: Policy Analysis and Research Programme of the Global Commission on International Migration.

de Bruijn, M., R. van Dijk and D. Foeken 2001. *Mobile Africa: changing patterns of movement in Africa and beyond.* Leiden, Boston: Brill Publishers.

de Haan, A. 2000. *Migrants, Livelihoods, and Rights: The Relevance of Migration in Development Policies.* London: Department for International Development (Social Development Working Paper; 4).

de Haas, H. 2006a. *Trans-Saharan Migration to North Africa and the EU: Historical Roots and Current Trends*, Migration Information Source (http://www.migration-information.org), November.

—— 2006b. *International migration and national development: Viewpoints and policy initiatives in countries of origin—The case of Nigeria.* Report prepared for Radboud University, Nijmegen and DGIS, Ministry of Foreign Affairs, The Netherlands.

—— 2007. *Morocco's migration experience: A transitional perspective*, International Migration (forthcoming).

Dixon, D. 2006. *Characteristics of the African Born in the United States*, Migration Information Source (http://www.migrationinformation.org), January.

Drumtra, J. 2003. *West Africa's Refugee Crisis Spills Across Many Borders*, Migration Information Source (http://www.migrationinformation.org), August.

Entzinger, H. 1985. *Return Migration in Western Europe*, International Migration 23 (2) 263–290.

Fargues, P. 2004. *Arab Migration to Europe: Trends and Policies*, International Migration Review 38 (4) 1348–1371.

—— (ed.) 2005. *Mediterranean Migration—2005 Report.* Cooperation project on the social integration of immigrants, migration, and the movement of persons. Financed by the EC MEDA Programme. Florence: EUI-RSCAS, CARIM Consortium.

Ferguson, J. 1999. *Expectations of Modernity: Myths and Meaning of Urban Life on the Zambian Copperbelt.* Berkeley CA: University of California Press.

Findley, S.E. 2004. *Mali: Seeking Opportunity Abroad*, Migration Information Source (http://www.migrationinformation.org), September.

Hamood, S. 2006. *African transit migration through Libya to Europe: the human cost.* Cairo: Forced Migration and Refugee Studies Program, American University of Cairo.

Hyndman, J. and B.V. Nylund 1998. *UNHCR and the Status of Prima Facie Refugees in Kenya*, International Journal of Refugee Law 10 (1–2) 21–48.

Iliffe, J. 1995 Africans: *The History of a Continent.* Cambridge: Cambridge University Press.

IOM 2000. *IOM Migration Policy Framework for Sub-Saharan Africa.* Geneva: International Organisation for Migration.

IOM 2005. *World Migration Report 2005: Costs and Benefits of Migration*, Vol. 3. Geneva: International Organisation for Migration.

IRIN 2003. *Ethiopia: ADB loan for tackling massive migration problem.* New York: United Nations Office for the Coordination of Humanitarian Affairs.

Katseli, L.T., R.E.B. Lucas and T. Xenogiani 2006. *Effects of Migration on Sending Countries: What do we know?* Paris: Organisation for Economic Co-operation and Development.

Kihato, C. and L.B. Landau 2006. *The Uncaptured Urbanite: Migration and State Power in Johannesburg.* Johannesburg: University of the Witwatersrand, Forced Migration Studies Programme (Forced Migration Working Paper Series).

Kress, B. 2006. *Burkina Faso: Testing the Tradition of Circular Migration*, Migration Information Source (http://www.migrationinformation.org), March.

Landau, L.B. 2004. *Myth and Decision in South African Migration Management and Research*. Johannesburg: University of the Witwatersrand, Forced Migration Studies Programme (Forced Migration Working Paper Series).

McDonald, D.A. and J. Crush (eds.) 2002. *Destinations Unknown: Perspectives on the Brain Drain in Southern Africa*. Pretoria: Africa Institute, SAMP.

Meillassoux, C. 1983. *The Economic Base of Demographic Reproduction: from the domestic mode of production to wage-earning*, Journal of Peasant Studies 11 (1) 50-61.

Miller, J.C. 1988. *Way of Death: Merchant capitalism and the Angolan slave trade 1730-1830*. Madison WI: University of Wisconsin Press.

Nugent, P. 1996. *Arbitrary Lines and the People's Minds: a dissenting view on colonial boundaries in West Africa*. In P. Nugent and A.I. Asiwaju (eds.) African Boundaries: Borders, Conduits and Opportunities. London: Pinter, 35–67.

OECD 2006. *The Web Atlas of Regional Integration in West Africa: Migration*. Paris: ECOWAS-SWAC / Organisation for Economic Co-operation and Development.

Peil, M. and P.O. Sada 1984. *African Urban Society*. Chichester: John Wiley and Sons.

Roe, E.M. 1995. *Except-Africa: Postscript to a special section on development narratives*, World Development 23 (6) 1065–1069.

Russell, S.S., K. Jacobsen and W.D. Stanley 1990. *International Migration and Development in Sub-Saharan Africa*. Washington D.C.: The World Bank.

Salih, R. 2001. *Moroccan Migrant Women: Transnationalism, Nation-States and Gender*, Journal of Ethnic and Migration Studies 27 (4) 655–671.

Sander, C. and S.M. Maimbo 2003. *Migrant Labor Remittances in Africa: Reducing Obstacles to Developmental Contributions*. Washington DC: The World Bank (Africa Region Working Paper Series).

Schmidley, A.D. 2001. *Profile of the Foreign-Born Population in the United States: 2000*. Washington DC: US Government Printing Office (US Census Bureau, Current Population Reports, Series P23–206).

Sell, R.R. 1988. *Egyptian International Labor Migration and Social Processes: Toward Regional Integration*, International Migration Review 22 (3) 87–108.

Stein, B.N. 1987. *ICARA II: Burden Sharing and Durable Solutions*. In J.R. Rogge (ed.) Refugees: A Third World Dilemma. New Jersey: Rowman and Littlefield.

Tornimbeni, C. 2005. *The state, labour migration and the transnational discourse—a historical perspective from Mozambique*, Wiener Zeitschrift für kritische Afrikastudien; Special Issue—African Migrations. Historical Perspectives and Contemporary Dynamics (8) 307–328.

UN 2006. *World Migrant Stock: The 2005 Revision Population Database*, Vol. 2006. New York: United Nations Population Division.

US DHS 2004. *Yearbook of Immigration Statistics 2003*. Washington DC: US Department of Homeland Security.

USCRI 2006. *World Refugee Survey 2006*. Washington DC: US Committee for Refugees and Immigrants.

Von Oppen, A. 1995. *Terms of Trade and Terms of Trust: the history and contexts of pre-colonial market production around the Upper Zambezi and Kasai*. Hamburg: Lit-Verlag.

White, C.M.N. 1960. *An Outline of Luvale Social and Political Organization*. Manchester: Manchester University Press (Rhodes-Livingstone Papers; 30).

Williams, V. and L. Carr 2006. *The Draft Protocol on the Facilitation of Movement of Persons in SADC: Implications for State Parties*. Kingston, Ontario: Southern African Migration Project (Migration Policy Brief; 18).

Wolpe, H. 1972. *Capitalism and Cheap Labour Power in South Africa: from segregation to apartheid*, Economy and Society 1 (4) 425–456.

Wright, C. 1995. *Gender Awareness in Migration Theory: synthesizing actor and structure in Southern Africa*, Development and Change 26, 771–791.

Zlotnik, H. 2003. *Imigrants' rights, forced migration and migration policy in Africa*. African Migration in Comparative Perspective. Johannesburg.

—— 2004. *International Migration in Africa: An Analysis Based on Estimates of the Migrant Stock*, Migration Information Source (http://www.migrationinformation.org), September.

Zohry, A. and B. Harrell-Bond 2003. *Contemporary Egyptian Migration: An Overview of Voluntary and Forced Migration.* Sussex: University of Sussex, Development Research Centre on Migration, Globalisation and Poverty.

MIGRATION AS RETERRITORIALIZATION: MIGRANT MOVEMENT, SOVEREIGNTY AND AUTHORITY IN CONTEMPORARY SOUTHERN AFRICA

Scarlett Cornelissen

Introduction

Conventionally, the way that power and sovereignty in the world system have been conceptualized in disciplines such as International Relations and International Political Economy (IPE) has been closely related to particular notions of territory and geographical space: power is seen to be that exercized by (legitimate or illegitimate) political authorities within contained geographical parameters; sovereignty pertains to the tacit and overt yielding to the existence of such geographic-political bodies by other like entities, and upon which the contriving of interaction on world scale occurs. The recent 'spatial turn' in social sciences has gone some way to disrupt what Agnew (1994) has lamented as the 'territorial trap' of the study of authority and power. Briefly, influenced by the move in philosophy and social sciences that emphasizes space not as a neutral container within which social relations occur, but as a constitutive element and active former of those social relations (cf. Lefebvre 1991), the 'spatial turn' has invited different conceptualizations of aspects such as state power. Seen in this frame space occupies and affects political societies; social groupings in turn act upon and create space(s); and entities such as the state can be viewed as manifestations of collective spatial imaginings which are not necessarily territorially bound. Instead, the state is a particular configuration of space upon which social relations are structured, meanings of sovereignty are assigned and political authority is based.

In tandem with this move toward changed understandings of statehood and power, concepts such as deterritorialization and reterritorialization have become widely ascribed to processes of altered state forms, in particular as reactions to globalization. Specifically, forces associated with globalization are seen to lead either to the weakening of state power and the attendant rise of alternative poles of political authority, economic or otherwise in form (deterritorialization) or to what scholars such as Brenner (2004) have termed the recalibration of state power (i.e. reterritorialization), where state authority is exercized in different guises and at different levels (such as through participation in international/supranational organizations or at substate level, such as through urban governance), but where, essentially the state continues to exercize a regulating influence on the movement of international capital.

Notions of the deterritorialization and/or reterritorialization of authority are useful for describing seemingly disparate processes of capitalist transformation and political shifts in the contemporary era. It is significant however, that what has developed into a rich and resourceful body of scholarship (e.g. Brenner 2004, Brenner et al. 2003, Evans 1997, Hazbun 2004, Ó Tuathail 2000) has tended to neglect how the decamping of the state, the resetting of authority and the reframing of territory are being affected by the current intensification of international mobility and population flows. Historically, migration has been a fundamental force in the formation and change not only of political territory, but also of societies. The *longue durée* of migration has been a persistent, if largely obscure shaper of nations, state territories and of cultures. In the contemporary era, however, migration across international boundaries has taken on a distinctive form, first in the increased pace with which such movement is able to occur, due in large part to globalization, and second in the political meaning that migration—in the effects it evokes from state authorities and societies—has taken on, as increasingly in receiving countries international relations become defined around convergent goals of stemming undesired population movements and preventing additional burdens on national fiscuses. More fundamentally, however, migration as a force unsettles well accepted and understood parameters of territory, and relatedly, political authority and identity (Appadurai 1996, Gupta and Ferguson 1992).

It is this relationship between migration, territory, power and sovereignty that forms the focus of this chapter. It is investigated how current-day shifts in authority in Southern Africa can be understood in terms of deterritorialization and reterritorialization and how migrant flows are a factor in such processes. In particular, it is examined how different types of migration regimes may be said to exist in the Southern African region, characterized by networks or interlinked chains of migrant movement, and the existence of migrant spaces that are separate from formal spheres of power. It is investigated what the impacts of these are on the political economy of the region. It is posited that migration is a discrete form of reterritorialization that is affecting political authority and state sovereignty in the region in distinct ways. Migrant movement and settlement affect economic and developmental processes in the region. More fundamentally however, such transit and settlement also present challenges to formal structures of state power at the intergovernmental, national and subnational levels. While state sovereignty and tied to it, physical features such as borders and delimited territory, have always been more adaptable and fluid in the African context, the way that such elements are being affected by an intensified regional migrant economy, is significant for showing out the disjuncture between attempts at the regional level to define the trappings of sovereignty (by for instance the sharpened defence of borders) and the general inefficacy of state jurisdiction. As a form of reterritorialization migration sees the creation of alternative economic and political spaces that raise the spectre of different forms and entities of political authority in the Southern African region.

   The first part of the chapter explores the interrelationship between migration, political spaces and territory in greater depth. This is done, first against the backdrop of the context of migration globally, and second, a review of the way that territory has been applied in scholarly analyses of political authority and statehood. The second part of the chapter reviews the contours of migration in the Southern African region, examining the main features, consequences and challenges posed by migrant flows in the region. Three forms of emergent and separate migrant regimes—formal-institutional, political and informal (defined by migrant spaces) are identified and discussed. The third and concluding part of the chapter extends the concept of this varied regional migrant regime and discusses some of the implications this poses for state sovereignty in the region.

Migration and political authority in the contemporary era

Five main trends in international migration

Increased mobility has become a key adjunct of the technological, economic and societal changes associated with late capitalism and the current phase of globalization. International tourist flows, which have risen rapidly over the past decade (to total 763 million arrivals in 2005; WTO 2005) are the quintessential example of the way that changes in socio-cultural values regarding leisure and associated travel, and socio-economic conditions have converged to propel the continued movement of people on a very large scale. As a form of migration international tourism has also gained significance as one of the largest and fastest growing sectors of the world economy. It is the crossing of borders on a more or less permanent basis, such as through emigration/immigration, refugee flows and displacement due to conflict, however, which has become a distinctive feature of international relations in the contemporary era, due to the political contexts and effects that such movements have. In this regard, the increased and predominant flow of people from the global South to North since the end of the Cold War, in search of better livelihood opportunities or fleeing from war, has prompted the establishment of policy regimes in major economic sites such as North America and Western Europe, which while aimed at curbing and controlling undesired population movements, have also laid the foundation for new kinds of political interaction between states of the North and South. Multilateral development assistance provided by the European Union (EU) to North African states over the past number of years, for example, have also sought to encourage those African states to exercize more rigid border controls (see, for example, *The Times*, 11 July 2006). Coarser means of engagement over migration flows have included the discussion in the EU a few years ago to establish transit processing centres (or asylum camps) within the territory of African sending states. In 2003 a proposal was made by the United Kingdom to develop such camps with the purpose of serving as catchment sites for asylum seekers and refugees deported from EU territory, and for would-be African migrants to the EU. The proposal was eventually rejected, but the idea of establishing refugee 'welcoming centres' extraterritorially of the EU is one which still holds currency.

While migration flows are highly variegated in form and mode—distinctions can be drawn between temporary and permanent movement; and examples of migrant movement can include sojourning, pilgrimage, or cross-border commuting—five main trends in current-day international migration may be discerned.[1]

---

[1] I am indebted to Giorgio Shani for this point.

First, it is possible today to speak of the globalization of migration, i.e. the increase both in the intensity and extent of international population movements, with a larger portion of world regions constituting both sites of migration origin and settlement. Statistics from the International Organization for Migration (IOM) indicate that migrant flows have substantially increased over the past decade, totalling 191 million in 2005, and that the number of countries both sending and receiving migrants has significantly grown. In geographical terms these figures emphasize the simultaneous and paradoxical dispersal and ellipsis so typical of globalization as a phenomenon. Socio-culturally, these statistics also hint to the more intense societal interactions and cultural pollination which theorists such as Castells (1997) and Appadurai (1996) describe.

Second, the pace of migration has accelerated. Prompted in large measure by the ability to be more mobile due to shifts in international socio-economic and technological conditions, but also in most major sending regions, circumstances of warfare or general desolation, the tempo by which migration has occurred, has significantly grown. The end of the Cold War, and the new geopolitical conditions which this event precipitated, accounts to a large degree for more intense flows of refugees and economic migrants from world regions such as Asia and Eastern Europe. In the African continent increased migrant flows, both within and across national borders relate closely to the stark proliferation in intra-state conflicts over the past 15 years.

The third predominant trend in international migration involves the increased distinction in the types of migrant flows, and in particular, the growth in economic migrancy. The number of refugees world wide has also increased, prompting a tightening of asylum policies in the regions of largest reception in North America and Western Europe.

Fourth, international migration has become increasingly feminized, with a growing number of women of different ages departing from their homes to search for work opportunities elsewhere. Studies of migration in Asia, indicating a stark change in the gender balance in population movements over the past number of years (e.g. UN 2005) parallel evidence from the African continent that a greater proportion of women are contributing to the steady growth of migrant flows in the continent (e.g. IOM 2005). The feminization of migration is accounted for by the loosening of many social strictures on female mobility and other cultural changes related, for instance to views on the social position of women and their economic role. Increasing adversity also encourages the greater feminization of population flows. In contexts such as Southern Africa, for example, weakened agricultural sectors affected by harsh and fluctuating climatic conditions have converged with changes in the composition of households due to the increasing incidence of Aids-related deaths, to necessitate on a growing scale the search for alternative livelihoods. The solution for many widows or girl children is to migrate from rural to urban areas within their own country or to the urban centres of other countries (Adepoju 2006). Within Southern Africa this new pattern of migration has replaced former predominant trends of labour migration that arose during the consolidation of apartheid in South Africa, but is built on established migrant labour routes emanating from this period, playing an augmentative role in furthering HIV infections in the region. In addition, the worldwide feminization of migration has gained a highly sinister dimension, as human trafficking and forced prostitution have also increased over the past number of years (Cross and Omoluabi 2006, IOM 2005).

The fifth major trend in international migration involves the manner in which migration has become a key factor in the determination of political agendas and priorities. This feature relates to three aspects: first, how specifically in net receiving countries, issues surrounding migration are central influences on the making of policy, and more noticeable over the past number of years in settings as diverse as Austria, the Netherlands, Sweden, Japan and the United States, perceptions regarding migration have shaped major domestic political outcomes such as electoral results. Second, this feature relates to how societal relations are increasingly also being framed by (often forced) interaction among migrant communities and host populations. The more intense politicization of such interactions over the past number of years has seen sometimes violent public remonstrations in countries such as France and the United Kingdom. This shaping of political identities and the entrenchment of societal divisions along distinctions of migrant and resident in net receiving countries relates closely to the third aspect of the political nature of international migration—how increasingly, migration as a phenomenon is used to mark out the identity of states and other state-related international actors, and how this comes to define international relations.

In this regard the example referred to above of the proposed transit processing centres has as much to do with the manner in which the European Union is seeking to delimit for itself a function and role as a political entity in the Westphalian system, partly through politico-juridical means and partly through instruments of disguised diplomatic coercion, as it has to do with the way in which this intergovernmental body seeks to consolidate its relationship with other states. Many other examples can be cited where convergent and collective policy-making on governing the movement of people, for stated economic and security reasons, has become an important singular thrust of international relations.

The example of the transit processing zones raises a further important aspect of the characteristics and disjunctures of international migration in the contemporary era, by drawing attention to the central position of 'territory', both in that territory constitutes the geographical latitude by which the movement of people gains context and meaning, but also in that state reactions to migration are defined in terms of territory. With regard to the latter point, the protection of state territory becomes a motivator for policy in a physical sense, manifesting in many receiving countries in the sharpened monitoring and defence of borders. Territory is also employed within states in a symbolic sense, where territory becomes synonymous with societal coherence and homogeneity, and by extension the survival and security of the state (Kumar 2003).

The territorial seclusion of the political unit which then was defined as the state by dominant social classes has been the main mechanism by which statehood historically has been forged (cf. Escolar 1997, Ruggie 1993). The early implementation of effective means of controlling and steering population movements within and outside of, at first abstract and later tangible borders, was a key component of this process. The nature of contemporary migration, however, evokes a different deployment of borders and territory in state rhetoric and apparatus. Recent policies and instruments adopted in the European Union (referred to above) are a case in point: through the use of various means of patrol and surveillance that are outsourced or externalized to migrant sending countries (such as North Africa), 'the border' and the responsibility for protecting it becomes shifted (Marvakis et al. 2006); in this process the 'territory' over which sovereignty is exercized is simultaneously extended and attenuated. It is in this way that migration can be said to create impulses where seemingly fixed and incontrovertible state zones, territories and borders become only liminal zones of international public interaction, and by which international relations increasingly are being shaped. As a force, migration however also invites different means of social identification, which in itself impacts on the way that political authority is formulated. It is to an exploration of the relationship between migration, territory and authority that the paper now briefly turns.

Migration and the deterritorialization and reterritorialization of power

The prominent role of territory in formal structures of international authority—state-centred or not—is a key point of departure in most scholarly analyses of the world system (Mann 1988). While this centrality of territory in scholarly understanding does pose its limitations (see Agnew 1994 for a cogent review), it does have certain epistemological advantages, such as drawing attention to the reflexive if invisible manner in which societal relations, and by extension institutions of power embed within self-selected territorial ranges. Territory, according to Berezin (2003: 7)

> ...is *social* because, independent of scale, persons inhabit it collectively; *political* because groups fight to preserve as well as to enlarge their space; and *cultural* because it contains the collective memories of its inhabitants. Territory is *cognitive* as well as physical, and its capacity to subjectify social, political and cultural boundaries makes it the core of public and private identity projects. Emotion is a constitutive dimension of territory [italics in original].

The territorialization of collective identity was a pivotal element of modern state formation (Anderson 1983, Calhoun 1997). In the context of globalization, it is now widely understood that alterations both in the physical form of territory and perceptions thereof, prompt different social orientations to territory. In this sense, Gupta and Ferguson's (1992: 68) claim that the contemporary world is one '...where identities are increasingly coming to be, if not wholly deterritorialized, at least differently territorialized,' is a useful description for the shifting involvement of social groupings with geographically defined political entities.

The way that academic scholarship has sought to relate to territory in the era of globalization, is embodied in the twin concepts of deterritorialization and reterritorialization, which have gained significant currency over the past number of years. In brief, deterritorialization encapsulates a set of claims over the decline of state authority in the contemporary world system, as alternative bodies of international

authority, such as multinational corporations or supranational organizations are assumed to subvert the autonomy and sovereignty of
the Westphalian state (Ohmae 1993). Reterritorialization can be seen
to be the counter to that process, involving the emergence of different scales of political community (e.g. Brenner 1998) or bases of
identification (e.g. Deleuze and Guattari 1987).

As concepts, however, deterritorialization and reterritorialization
are used in widely varying ways in scholarship. Ó Tuathail's (2000: 139)
depiction of deterritorialization as 'the name given to the problematic
of territory losing its significance and power in everyday life,' is a
broad and for this reason representative definition of a phenomenon
which for some would lead to the complete eclipse of the Westphalian
inter-state system (e.g. Held 1995), the loosening of the grip of nation-
identity (Appadurai 2003), the declining significance of location for
economic decision-making (Ohmae 1993) and the increased separation
between politico-economic units and territory. Reterritorialization
is generally posited as the opposite of that whereby territory is not
seen to lose its importance, but where it becomes a container for
political and economic relations in forms other than that of the state.
Significantly, therefore, predominant usages of reterritorialization
tacitly accept arguments about the curbed and eventually shrunken
away position of the state.

There is an emergent strand in the reterritorialization discourse,
however, which also characterizes this process as one whereby state
sovereignty is remoulded and channelled through alternative paths
of influence, and through which the state maintains a hand in the
regulation of capital. Hazbun's (2004: 319) depiction of the active role
of the state in reconfiguring 'control over ... (territorial and national)
resources ... and the generation of territorial rents and externalities,'
whereby firms are for instance encouraged through the use of policy
instruments to invest or operate from a given location, is representative of this analysis. In this, the state is viewed as one among a
multitude of economic actors that influence the international movement of capital; the state, however, also helps to establish the broader
regulatory parameters for the creation and exchange of capital. As
such, while absolute sovereignty in the making of fiscal policy may
be affected by globalization, states can and do still exercize influence
over the wider flow of capital. Regionalization, incentives to promote
firm clustering or agglomeration, the encouragement of industries
that are consumption-driven (such as urban-based fashion or design

centres or tourism) or of industries that are geographically less fixed (such as the Information and Communications Technology sector) are all part of a repertoire of state instruments to influence the national and international geography of capital.

Brenner (2004) has analyzed the rising significance of cities in the world economy, and the increased role played by urban authorities in the governance of capital, as a further component of reterritorialization. His is part of a wider discourse that has started to develop in IPE that examines how, centred around cities, state sovereignty can be redefined to coincide not necessarily with territorial borders, but as the means whereby the state engages and adapts with a changing international environment. In this frame, cities (particularly those of the world or global order magnitude) are at times salient points around which international economic relations converge and are steered, but, at times the containers by which state interactions are calibrated and through which national states can give form to policy goals (e.g. Cerny 2003, Jessop 2002, Weiss 1998). Brenner (2004) is representative of an emerging approach to state sovereignty when he characterizes the growing importance of cities as indicative of a 'rescaling of statehood': the process by which national states align institutions of policy-making and regulation with or through sub-national and supranational bodies, and as a result continue to influence international outcomes.

It is useful to regard deterritorialization and reterritorialization as constitutive and dialectical components of constant processes of international economic restructuring (Brenner 1998). In this view, globalization is part of an extended course whereby capitalistic arrangements are moulded by certain institutional and societal conditions and manifest in certain geographical forms, but are also continuously changed as those institutional and societal configurations change (Harvey 1985). In this sense, power and political authority should be considered both in the manner in which it exhibits in the exercize of state control, and in the way in which other economic and societal bodies (such as firms, communities or social movements) organize and express as autonomous actors, and have political impact.

Taken as an independent force, international migration relates in interesting ways to the dialectic of deterritorialization and reterritorialization at the international scale and the way that these processes are studied. First, it necessitates fluid understanding of 'territory,' which could be physical, formal, informal or representational. Migrant flows unsettle and expand fixed geographical edges, but also interrupt the coincidence of spheres of collective consciousness (manifesting in national or group identity) with specific territories. Second, and relatedly migration is both prompted by but also stimulates distinctive subjectivities that are fashioned within spatial spheres that have little to do with state territories. Third, at the institutional level, and following Harvey (1985, 1991) migration may be viewed as a particular force of 'creative destruction' that affects the capitalist foundation of the world economy in particular ways, influencing the prevailing economic and political institutions within which capitalism as a mode of accumulation embeds.

Appadurai (1996) has provided a highly cogent analysis of the overlay between migration and capitalism (or modernity, in his terms) in the contemporary era and the dialectic influence of the first on the second. Modernity, according to Appadurai rests on the creation and simultaneous rupture of a particular collective imagination. The use, dispersal and consumption of symbols through the intervening influence of mass media, along with cultural dissemination associated with mass migration, are for Appadurai two main means whereby modernity is propelled, and globalization as a contemporary facet of modernity, formed and adapted in diverse social settings. Appadurai (1996: 33–36) identifies five dominant forms of electronically mediated and mobility-shaped global cultural flows: a) *ethnoscapes*, 'the landscape of persons who constitute the shifting world in which we live: tourists, immigrant, refugees, exiles, guest workers and other moving groups'; b) *technoscapes*, 'the global configuration, also ever fluid, of technology'; c) *mediascapes*, 'the distribution of the electronic capabilities to produce and disseminate information…and the images of the world created by these media'; d) *ideoscapes*, which 'are also concatenations of images, but they are often directly political and frequently have to do with the ideologies of states and the counter-ideologies of movements explicitly oriented to capturing state power or a piece of it'; and e) *financescapes*, constituted of the diverse bodies of organizations, markets and agencies that produce and regulate international finances.

Taken together, these five 'landscapes' comprise the international political economy and are in effect structures whereby international authority is either constituted (such as the financescape and the ideoscape) or adapted and ameliorated (such as the mediascapes and technoscapes). Appadurai's depiction is useful for laying emphasis on the relational and disjunctive nature of international structures of authority. It is also important for stressing the production of authority, a process which requires the continuous and affirmative construction of institutions of control and which relies for its existence on the successful stimulation of societal assent (Lefebvre 1991).

Most useful in Appadurai's analysis for this chapter is, through his identification of ethnoscapes, the stress on the temporality and spatial fluidity of social collections that affect structures of power. Migrant flows create migrant spaces that relate to or disengage with predominant edifices of authority in host societies. Also, territories, political or otherwise, become sites of negotiation for populations on the move, either in their attempts to adjust to new environments, or to adapt such environments to their accustomed social practices. Political authority, in other words, is affected and modified in significant ways by migrant flows.

The political economy of migration in Southern Africa

The context

In one sense, migration has long been a predominant feature of African societies, and demographic and associated political change on the African continent can be viewed as an enduring process of movement and settlement, marked by elemental events such as slavery, colonialism and state formation, but in totality, the *longue durée* of population shifts on the continent has been undulating and a constant element in the shaping of African political economy (Mafukidze 2006). In the contemporary era, however, migration has gained an added, more explicitly economic dimension, influenced in direct and indirect fashions by wider international processes. The context of conflict and the intensified struggle over resources in the current-day frame, should be viewed as adding to the effects of shifts in the international political economy.

Within Southern Africa, migration has become one of the most predominant factors in the reshaping of this region's socio-economic and socio-political environments. The political economy of migration in Southern Africa is one which historically, has been driven by distinct forms of industrialization shaped by colonialism and related processes of state formation, and the heavy, spatially mediating impact of apartheid policies. In this context, migration was associated with social disruption and haemorrhage and from a statist perspective, one element in a tight arrangement of sovereignty, security, social movement and constraint.

The end of apartheid introduced a different momentum to population movements in the region. Changes to both the political meaning and policy approach to migration in the Southern African region followed after the end of apartheid, propelled by a strong 'redress ideology' in the policy goals of the new South African government which were transported to that government's stance to regional migration and development. Migration now came to be viewed as an important component of attempts to foster regional development and the establishment of economic and other types of equity in the region. Migration patterns in Southern Africa have followed much the same direction as flows in other parts of the world, marked first, by a general upward surge in population movement and second a strong increase in rural-to-urban migration. As in most other developing countries, urbanization has been a predominant force in Southern Africa's political economy, bringing with it an own attendant set of development issues and challenges. Table 1 illustrates the level of migration in a selected number of Southern African countries while Table 2 indicates the levels of urbanization in the main cities in these countries over the same period.

What is not captured in the tables below, is the level of cross-border movement in Southern Africa, which both of a temporary and permanent nature, has increased since the end of the Cold War and the move to democratization in South Africa. Underpinning this increased flow is a complex mix of political and economic forces and impulses. Lengthy periods of intra-state conflict in the Lusophone countries have made population displacement—within and across the borders—an almost constant feature of these countries. The demographic features of neighboring countries have concomitantly been affected. By one estimate for example, more than 120,000 Angolans are currently living in western Central Zambia. The greater portion of these people has settled more or less permanently in Zambia, integrating with the local population (Okamoto 2002). The end of the war in Angola has, however, also prompted a steady flow of returnees to that country. Similarly, continuous circular movement between the Democratic Republic of Congo (DRC) and Zambia is accounted for by cycles of violence and non-violence in the DRC.

Table 1. Changes in immigrant populations in a selected
number of Southern African countries

	Botswana	Lesotho	Namibia	South Africa	Swaziland
1976					
Percentage of total population	1.6	0.4	4.5	3.7	5.4
Number	13,000	4,000	42,000	962,000	28,000
1986					
Percentage of total population	1.7	1.1	7.4	5.5	5.8
Number	20,000	16,000	84,000	1,815,000	41,000
1996					
Percentage of total population	2.4	0.3	7.5	3.3	4.0
Number	38,000	5,000	124,000	1,353,000	38,000
2003					
Percentage of total population	3.0	0.3	7.5	3.0	4.0
Number	52,000	6,000	143,000	1,303,000	42,000

Source: Adapted from UN, 2003.

Since 1994, population flows in several other Southern African countries were influenced by the attempts of the post-apartheid government in South Africa to consolidate the foreign migrant population in that country. In 1995 and again in 1996 an amnesty process was implemented whereby undocumented labour migrants, mainly miners, and people from other states of the Southern African Development Community (SADC) could gain permanent residence status. This process of amnesty was an early effort on the part of the post-apartheid government to establish the number of undocumented migrants in the country and to acquire a grip on illegal immigrant flows. The amnesty process was largely unsuccessful in this regard (Crush and Williams 1999), although it did constitute an initial part of a migration policy in South Africa which has largely been mottled and counterproductive (Crush 2006). In its attempts to ameliorate population settlement, the amnesty process was also part of the

Table 2. Urban populations in selected Southern African cities

	Botswana	Lesotho	Namibia	South Africa	Swaziland
1976					
Annual rural population growth (%)	2.5	1.6	2.2	2.5	1.8
Annual urban population growth (%)	12.6	6.7	4.8	2.7	10.1
Urban population proportion (%)	13	11	21	48	14
2003					
Annual rural population growth (%)	-0.3	-0.4	0.9	-1.1	0.4
Annual urban population growth (%)	1.4	3.4	3.3	2.1	2.2
Urban population proportion (%)	50	30	32	59	27

Source: Adapted from UN, 2003.

strong focus on changing the spatial effects of apartheid, that has characterized much of post-apartheid policy-making. Nonetheless, returnee labour migrants from the mid-1990s, encouraged by migration initiatives undertaken by the South African government, have contributed to a not insignificant cross-border flow between South Africa and its neighbouring countries.

The strongest direction for cross-border movement since the end of apartheid, however, has been toward South Africa. The greatest impulse for this is economic, as people from several other parts of the African continent search for better livelihood opportunities. Estimates of the size of the undocumented immigrant population in South Africa vary widely, ranging from between 2 million and 5 million, as claimed by the South African government and bodies such as the Human Sciences Research Council (e.g. Minnaar and Hough 1996) and (a highly improbable) 12 million, as claimed by some civil society groups (such as opposition political parties). Both official and unofficial estimates and discourses around this issue are telling for the level of chauvinism that they convey. Xenophobia has become a social problem in South Africa, and incidences of violence against immigrants, often resulting in murder, have steadily increased over the past number of years.[2] Popular discourse, carried through by the media, sees immigrants from other African countries blamed for violent crime, unemployment, poverty and other social ills in South Africa (see, for instance, McDonald and Jacobs 2005). The use by the government of terms such as 'illegal alien,' a term that is institutionally sanctioned through policy, and reportedly harsh treatment of immigrants by the South African police and border officials, cynically add to the unfavourable position of immigrants in the country.

Data on migrant flows in Southern Africa, as in other parts of the world, are notoriously deficient. Aside from the fact that documenting the movement of peoples who wish to be invisible is near to impossible, the very process of documentation is a political one, as illustrated above. Regional cross-border movement into South Africa of a temporary nature is however captured in statistics that document daily border crossings, and (inappropriately) are depicted as tourism movement. General tourism statistics captured at South Africa's main border posts, while aiming to gauge the number of leisure travelers from Southern Africa countries into South Africa, indeed predominantly capture the flow of people who seek to find employment, trade or shop in South Africa. While representing only a fraction of cross-border movement into South Africa, it does provide some indication of the general pattern of such movement. Data that are officially captured as intra-Southern African tourism statistics, therefore, do constitute a point of reference for cross-border flows. The greatest level of cross-border movement exists between Lesotho and South Africa, although entry into the country from Botswana and Mozambique, and over the past number of years, Zimbabwe, is also significant.

---

[2] As an illustration of the extent of this problem, for several months during 2006 more than 10 Somali merchants and shop owners trading in townships in the Western Cape province were killed during what appears to be an orchestrated campaign by organized elements from the host communities.

Table 3. International cross-border arrivals into South Africa

Year	Total international arrivals (number)	Overseas arrivals		African arrivals	
		Number	Share of total (%)	Number	Share of total (%)
1993	3,093,183	618,637	20	2,474,546	80
1994	3,668,956	704,439	19.2	2,964,516	80.8
1995	4,488,272	1,072,697	23.9	3,415,575	76.1
1996	4,944,430	1,171,829	23.7	3,772,601	76.3
1997	4,976,349	1,273,945	25.6	3,702,404	74.4
1998	5,732,039	1,427,277	24.9	4,304,762	75.1
1999	5,917,700	1,491,260	25.2	4,426,440	74.8
2000	5,900,000	1,528,100	25.9	4,371,900	74.1
2001	5,787,368	1,502,090	26*	4,134,141	71*
2002	6,429,583	1,803,887	28*	4,455,971	69*

* Difference accounted for by unspecified entries.
Source: Statistics South Africa.

The emergence of a migration regime in Southern Africa

While it is difficult to rely on surveys and official statistics on migrant flows of any nature to draw conclusions on the size and extent of Southern African migration, such data do portray general tendencies, which in turn carry some implication for the region's wider political economy. In this regard three main features may be isolated. The first concerns the closer interlinking of Southern African states into a regional migration network. Population movement that is of a circuitous nature entwine the region's economies in ways that are not yet completely understood. Related to this, the second feature concerns the development of a migration regime, which is operative at a formal level, through the introduction of several national and regional institutional instruments of collaboration, but also at an informal level, in the form, for instance, of informal economic activities that straddle different national territories. The third feature encapsulates the other two, and involves the fashioning of migrant spaces that both as transnational and localized spaces, affect the exercize of power and parameters of sovereignty in the region.

A migration regime may be defined in an institutional sense, following Krasner (1983) according to the predominant norms, values and goals that are common to the political actors participating in

the regime, and the organizational arrangements by which cooperation among the actors is shaped. In this way a migration regime is a
formal expression of collectively determined objectives concerning
the regulation of the movement of people. In the Southern Africa
region such formal institutional articulation has started to take shape
in the various attempts to converge economic and political policy-
making, and through the expansion of the SADC. Within the SADC this
is firstly observable in the increased movement toward integration
most concretely reflected in the decision made in 1996 to establish
an area of free trade and labor movement. The rationale for this is
to a large part economic, with the assumption that coherence may
be encouraged through the establishment of a free trade area, and
that this may lead to increased regional trade. In turn, it is assumed
that this trade could encourage the evening out of regional economic
disparities (Takirambudde 1999).

The regulation of economic exchange is also aimed at influencing
the macroeconomic conditions within SADC member states, with the
goal of improving the general level of development in those countries,
and indirectly, reducing economic migrant flows. Other indirect means
of regulating populations with the goal of directing the flow of capital
include the use of spatial mechanisms such as Spatial Development
Initiatives and relatedly, export processing zones. More direct attempts
at regulating regional migration within the structures of SADC involve
efforts to develop a common migration policy. Little success has been
achieved with these efforts, in large part due to the organizational
inadequacies of SADC itself.

Given that the predominant direction of migration within the
region is into South Africa, the content of this country's migration
policy and the efficacy with which such policy is drawn up and
implemented, may be said to play an inordinately influential role in
the success with which migration policy in SADC is enacted. In this
sense a second way of characterizing a Southern African migration
regime—as the active production of physical and symbolic borders—is
relevant. Borders may be viewed both as institutions and as processes
(Anderson 1996). As an institution a border encamps and demarcates
the territory to which state identity is attached and by which state
sovereignty is claimed. As a process borders fulfil the role of matching
the exercize of statehood, through policies and various other forms of
statecraft, with official discourses that seek to establish cultural and

societal cohesiveness. In this way borders, 'and their related narratives of frontiers, (are) indispensable elements in the construction of national cultures,' and identity (Donnan and Wilson 1999: 5). Borders are therefore maintained physically, but also representationally. This latter point is important, since it emphasizes once again the flexible way that territory and borders can be used by states as they go along in their business of security and protection: the 'border' is anywhere the state seeks to defend the polity. In the aftermath of 9/11, the initiation of the so-called 'global war against terror' and the establishment of various institutions of state surveillance (such as in the United States the Department of Homeland Security and similar agencies of monitoring and control in EU states such as Europol and the Schengen Information System), the geographical and abstract extension of the 'border' has become particularly exaggerated.

The meaning and physical content of borders in Southern Africa are vastly different to that in the North. In large measure this is due to the lack of capacity and infrastructure to screen, regulate and contain regional population movements. Given this, proposals have been put forward in SADC to establish regional mechanisms of population control through amongst others, camps for asylum seekers and an electronic database that captures biographical data on all cross-border movements. Although some way off, if migrant, asylum or refugee camps were to be established and operated on a regional basis, they would constitute *de facto* new border regions which not only would affect the flow of people in Southern Africa, but would also have implications for the foundation upon which territorial claims are made by Southern African states. The meaning not only of borders, but of statehood within Southern Africa would be altered.

Borders relate to the regional migration regime also in a symbolic manner, in the way in which state narratives around the protection of borders serve to inculcate specific, negative views on immigrants in the region. In a perceptive review, Landau (2006) provides account of several prevailing 'myths' around migrants and migration that shape policy-making in South Africa. Central of these are claims furthered by the South African state itself, of the 'deluge' of 'illegal aliens' and the burden they place on a fiscus which is already stretched and on a society with its own developmental imperatives. Landau cites a speech by the first post-apartheid minister of Home Affairs, Mangosuthu Buthelezi, who stated:

> If we as South Africans are going to compete for scarce resources with
> millions of aliens who are pouring into South African, then we can bid
> goodbye to our Reconstruction and Development Programme (cited in
> Landau 2006: 230).

Such narratives have the effect of laying the idea of the 'border'
centrally in citizens' minds, transforming what is a physical mani-
festation of power into something symbolic. The state draws its own
claims to sovereignty from such symbolic constructions. It is in this
sense that a Southern African migration regime has evolved that is
pivotally representational in nature, and through which states seek
to produce and reclaim their own authority in the region.

There is a third sense in which a Southern African migration regime
could be delineated, however, which yields different conclusions on
the health of state power and sovereignty in the region. This relates
to the spaces that migrants themselves create both in the means and
routes by which they transit and in their patterns of settlement. The
fact that large numbers of migrants are able to escape detection by
institutions of state control of varying sophistication, and that they
are able to traverse borders with apparent ease, also means that
migrants escape (or better, are not observed by) formal structures of
political authority. Once settled, migrants also create their own spaces
that at points may interrelate with spaces of host societies, but at
others may be completely separate from it. The case of South Africa
provides illustration of how migrant economic spaces have arisen in
the key urban centres of Johannesburg, Durban and to a lesser extent
Cape Town, which have transformed sizeable parts of these cities (e.g.
Rogerson 1998). In these cities settlement by migrants from the rest
of the African continent has had some effect on the spatial economy,
with migrants typically partaking in trading activities and contributing to the growth of the so-called second economy (Rogerson 1996,
Rogerson and Rogerson 1997).

One further characteristic of emergent migrant spaces in places
such as South Africa's inner cities, is the stark distinction between
'formal' and 'informal' spheres of political exchange, with migrants
(like the poor, more generally) excluded from the central institutions
through which power is exercized. Formal structures of power, however, are impinged upon by migrants, their movements and the spaces
that they occupy. Development policy by urban authorities in South
Africa, for instance, increasingly is oriented toward if not accommodating immigrants, reacting to and taking shape around the economic

and social impacts that they leave (Landau 2006). While therefore not able to participate in formal channels of politics, migrants maintain a political force. It is in this way that migrants also challenge established domains of authority.

If it is accepted that migrant movement creates alternative (informal) spaces in Southern Africa, then it is also clear that the transnational networks, remittance economies and diaspora communities that migrants found constitute separate sites of subjectivity, and importantly, alternative regimes of authority. The intensification of migration as phenomenon therefore, carries implications for sovereignty in the Southern African region. While the relationship between territory and sovereignty in the African setting has always been of an aberrant nature in the Westphalian frame—with borders marked by physical and abstract fluidity, and authority characteristically more sinuous, adaptable and varied—it can be posited that migration in its current form stimulates the reframing of authority, precisely because it shows out the paradoxes and limitations of attempts to maintain territorially defined statehood, within a context in which territory has assumed different political meaning. Migration also stimulates alternative economic bases, which may subvert formal establishments of authority. Landau (2005) has for instance described the emergence of 'zones of exception' in urban South Africa where 'economies of corruption' have emerged around the trafficking of contraband, but also sinisterly, the extension of illegal documentation to migrants by state officials.

Conclusion: Migration's challenges to territory and power

A result of the heavy Weberian influence in political and sociological theory is that ideas about state power have customarily centred, albeit in diverse ways, on territory. In general, territorialization was seen as the physical process by which not only the geographical parameters of the state were set, but importantly, the means of state security—the *raison d'être*—were defined. The wide-ranging impact of globalization in the contemporary era has invited a different deployment of the position of territory in scholarly works on statehood, with deterritorialization portrayed as a reactive process to the loss of state power, and reterritorialization used to refer to novel (territory-less) forms of power. Given that migration is a process which is essentially about geography, movements across and impacts upon territory, it is interesting that the relationship between migration and authority has not been extensively explored in what is an otherwise steadily growing body of scholarship on power in the contemporary era. In essence, both in process and through effect, migration can be seen as an instance both of deterritorialization and reterritorialization, that affects the way that authority, formal and informal is constituted and put into effect. At the world level, international migration can be viewed as a process that exercizes a dialectical influence on formal state-level structures of power, inviting in certain contexts alterations in state authority.

This seems to play out in current-day Southern Africa to a significant extent. Migration has always been a constant feature and significant factor in the creation of communities and the transformation of state power in this region. In the contemporary era, however, migration in the region displays particular traits—it is increasing and more extensive in scope, and a greater politico-economic force than had heretofore been the case. These features result directly from political changes in the region, and relatedly, alterations in state power. At the same time, migrant flows have the effect of further challenging and in some instances weakening states' capacities of exercising jurisdiction. Migration also sees the emergence of alternative sites of authority which at times may coincide with formal institutions of authority linked to specific territories, and at other points not.

Migration may therefore be said to be a distinct process of reterritorialization that is shaping the nature of power in the Southern African region. What the further impacts of this process may be, and what the implications for authority will be, will to a large measure depend on the way that wider international political and economic factors affect the Southern African region. As a force of reterritorialization migration will also invite different means of political exchange in the region that will require further research. Three areas may be suggested. First, the extent to which formal processes of political participation is adapted to include migrant settlement communities, and axiomatically how forms of political expression could be read through various types of agency within migrant communities; second, the nature of the political economy created by migrant trading activities and how this interrelates with or contribute to established national and regional economies; and finally, the nature of and distinctions within migrant subjectivities around which economic and other social spaces are created, how these relate to host societies, and what this suggests for the way in political authority is newly comprised.

References

Adepojou, A. 2006. *Leading issues in international migration in sub-Saharan Africa*. In C. Cross et al. (eds.) Views on Migration in sub-Saharan Africa: Proceedings of an African Migration Alliance Workshop. Pretoria: HSRC Press, 25–47.

Agnew, J. 1994. *The territorial trap: the geographical assumptions of international relations theory*, Review of International Political Economy (1) 53–80.

Anderson, B. 1983. *Imagined communities: reflections on the origin and spread of nationalism*. London: Verso.

Anderson, M. 1996. *Frontiers: Territory and State Formation in the Modern World*. Oxford: Polity.

Appadurai, A. 1996. *Modernity at Large: Cultural Dimensions of Globalization*. Minneapolis: University of Minnesota Press.

—— 2003. *Sovereignty without territoriality: Notes for a postnational geography*. In S.M. Low and D. Lawrence-Zúniga (eds.) The Anthropology of Space and Place. Locating Culture. Oxford: Blackwell, 337–349.

Berezin, M. 2003. *Introduction—Territory, emotion and identity: spatial recalibration in a new Europe*. In M. Berezin and M. Schain (eds.) Europe Without Borders: Remapping Territory, Citizenship and Identity in a Transnational Age. Maryland: Johns Hopkins University Press, 1–32.

Brenner, N. 1998. *Between fixity and motion: accumulation, territorial organization and the historical geography of spatial scales*, Environment and Planning D: Society and Space (16) 459–481.

—— 2004. *New state spaces: Urban governance and the rescaling of statehood*. Oxford: Oxford University Press.

—— et al. (eds.) 2003. *State/Space: A Reader*. Oxford: Blackwell.

Calhoun, C. 1997. *Nationalism*. Minneapolis: University of Minnesota Press.

Castells, M. 1997. *The Power of Identity*. Oxford: Blackwell.

Cerny, P. 2003. *What next for the state?* In E. Kofman and G. Youngs (eds.) Globalization: Theory and Practice. 2nd ed. London: Continuum, 207–221.

Cross, C. and E. Omoluabi 2006. *Introduction*. In C. Cross et al. (eds.) Views on Migration in sub-Saharan Africa: Proceedings of an African Migration Alliance Workshop. Pretoria: HSRC Press, 1–24.

Crush, J. 2006. *States of Vulnerability: the Future Brain Drain of Talent to South Africa*. Cape Town: Southern African Migration Project.

Crush, J. and V. Williams (eds.) 1999. *The New South Africans? Immigration Amnesties and their Aftermath*. Cape Town: Idasa and the Southern African Migration Project.

Deleuze, G. and F. Guattari 1987. *A Thousand Plateaus: Capitalism and Schizophrenia*. Minneapolis: University of Minnesota Press.

Donnan, H. and T.M. Wilson 1999. *Borders: Frontiers of Identity, Nation and State*. New York: Berg.

Escolar, M. 1997. *Exploration, cartography and the modernization of state power*, International Social Science Journal (151) 55–76.

Evans, P. 1997. *The eclipse of the state? Reflections on stateness in an era of globalization*, World Politics (50) 62–87.

Gupta, A. and J. Ferguson 1992. *Beyond 'culture': space, identity and the politics of difference*, Cultural Anthropology 71 (1) 6–23.

Harvey, D. 1985. *The geopolitics of capitalism.* In D. Gregory and J. Urry (eds.) Social Relations and Spatial Structures. London: Macmillan, 128–163.
––––– 1991. *The Condition of Postmodernity.* Oxford: Blackwell.
Hazbun, W. 2004. *Globalisation, reterritorialisation and the political economy of tourism development in the Middle East,* Geopolitics 9 (2) 310–341.
Held, D. 1995. *Democracy and the Global Order: From the Modern State to Cosmopolitan Governance.* Cambridge: Polity.
IOM 2005. *World Migration 2005: Costs and Benefits of International Migration.* Geneva: International Organization for Migration.
Jessop, B. 2002. *The Future of the Capitalist State.* London: Polity.
Krasner, S. (ed.) 1983. *International Regimes.* London: Cornell University Press.
Kumar, K. 2003. *The idea of Europe: cultural legacies, transnational imaginings and the nation-state.* In M. Berezin and M. Schain (eds.) Europe Without Borders: Remapping Territory, Citizenship and Identity in a Transnational Age. Maryland: Johns Hopkins University Press, 33–50.
Landau, L. 2005. *Urbanisation, nativism, and the rule of law in South Africa's 'forbidden cities,* Third World Quarterly 26 (7) 1115–1134.
––––– 2006. *Myth and rationality in Southern African responses to migration, displacement, and humanitarianism.* In C. Cross et al. (eds.) Views on Migration in Sub-Saharan Africa: Proceedings of an African Migration Alliance Workshop. Pretoria: HSRC Press, 220–244.
Lefebvre, H. 1991. *The Production of Space.* Oxford: Blackwell.
Mafukidze, J. 2006. *A discussion of migration and migration patterns and flows in Africa.* In C. Cross et al. (eds.) Views on Migration in Sub-Saharan Africa: Proceedings of an African Migration Alliance Workshop. Pretoria: HSRC Press, 103–129.
Mann, M. 1988. *States, War and Capitalism: Studies in Political Sociology.* Oxford: Blackwell.
Marvakis, A., D. Parsonoglou and V. Tsianios 2006. *Rebordering Europe.* Paper presented at Colloquium on 'Transnationalism, Migrant Spaces and Citizenship—Perspectives from Africa and Europe,' Stellenbosch, South Africa, 20 November.
McDonald, D.A. and S. Jacobs 2005. *(Re)writing xenophobia: understanding press coverage of cross-border migration in Southern Africa,* Journal of Contemporary African Studies 23 (3) 295–325.
Minnaar, A. and M. Hough 1996. *Who Goes There? Perspectives on Clandestine and Illegal Aliens in Southern Africa.* Pretoria: HSRC Publishers.
Ó Tuathail, G. 2000. *Borderless worlds? Problematising discourses of deterritorialisation.* In N. Kliot and D. Newman (eds.) Geopolitics at the End of the Twentieth Century: The Changing World Political Map. London: Frank Cass.
Ohmae, K. 1993. *The rise of the region-state,* Foreign Affairs 72 (2) 78–87.
Okamoto, M. 2002. *The subsistence system in Lozi society on the Zambezi River Floodplain,* Asian and African Area Studies (2) 193–242.
Rogerson, C. 1996. *Dispersion within concentration: the changing location of corporate headquarter offices in South Africa,* Development Southern Africa 13 (4) 567–579.
––––– 1998. *High-technology clusters and infrastructure development: international and South African experiences,* Development Southern Africa 15 (5) 875–906.
––––– and J. Rogerson 1997. *The changing post-apartheid city: emergent black-owned small enterprises in Johannesburg,* Urban Studies 34 (1) 85–103.
Ruggie, J.G. 1993. *Territoriality and beyond: problematizing modernity in international relations,* International Organization 47 (1) 139–174.
Takirambudde, P. 1999. *The rival strategies of SADC and PTA/COMESA.* In D. Bach (ed.) Regionalisation in Africa: Integration and Disintegration. Oxford: James Curry, 151–158.

UN 2003. *World Population Policies 2003*. New York: UN Department of Economic and Social Affairs.
UN 2005. *Trends in Total Migrant Stock: The 2005 Revision*. Geneva: United Nations.
Weiss, L. 1998. *The Myth of the Powerless State*. Ithaca, NY: Cornell University Press.
WTO 2005. *Tourism Highlights*. Madrid: World Tourism Organisation.

APPROACHING AFRICAN TOURISM:
PARADIGMS AND PARADOXES

Walter van Beek

> *Travel will do you good by giving you knowledge of*
> *people, shapes of mountains,*
> *plains extending to unknown lengths,*
> *valleys with eternal waters trickling through,*
> *[but] you will not become better or more sensible.*
> Seneca[1]

Introduction

Tourism has old roots. At the start of the first millennium Seneca noted the urge of people to see foreign lands and strange landscapes, and, true to his vocation, he felt compelled to write his wry commentaries, serving as the first known elitist critique of the phenomenon. From the start the elite seem to have frowned upon the idea of traveling for fun; after all, the word 'travel' stems from '*travail*', the verb work, so from a serious business. The oldest known European system of tourism was called pilgrimage, serious religious business if anything. Yet, already in that age the enjoyment of travel sometimes superseded religious motivations. In 1076 AD another early critic of tourism, Jacques de Vitry, wrote

> Some light minded people go on pilgrimages not out of devotion but out of mere curiosity and love of novelty. All they want to do is to travel through unknown lands to investigate the absurd, often exaggerated, stories they have heard about the east (cited in Smith and Brent 2001: 4).

Chaucer's Canterbury Tales, one of the early masterpieces of European literature, is set in a pilgrimage setting itself,[2] and some characters, such as the wife of Bath, have been to all major pilgrimage centres in

---

[1] Roman philosopher and playwright, 4 BC–55 AD.
[2] To the grave of Thomas Becket, in Canterbury.

Europe, including Jerusalem. Pilgrimage is for forgiveness and holiness, but also for amusement. And the Tales surely are amusing.

After the pilgrimages—which still are an important stimulus for tourism even to this very day—the torch of tourism was carried by the Grand Tour, the essential education for an English gentleman of ample means in the seventeenth and eighteenth century, in fact till the advent of the steam train. A trip through France, Switzerland, Italy, Germany and the Low countries was the ideal way of preparing for a life in diplomacy or studied leisure, but, of course, like most pilgrimages, it was only for the happy few who could afford it. Still, this kind of tourism also had its critics. The Grand Tour was said to re-enforce the old preconceptions and prejudices concerning national characteristics, as Jean Gailhard's *Compleat Gentleman* (1678) observes: 'French courteous. Spanish lordly. Italian amorous. German clownish.'

The first tour guides already appear in the late Middle Ages, with detailed information on what inns to frequent and what inn keepers to avoid. Travel gently developed from a necessity imposed by either religion or education, to an integral part of one's social *persona*. Already the early pilgrim and, surely, the gentleman-at-leisure could ill afford *not* to undertake a pilgrimage or tour; the education of a gentleman was simply not advanced without exposure to the great works of ancient times and a thorough glimpse at the Renaissance of Southern Europe; and a wealthy catholic patron who had never been to one of the many holy sites, was lacking in faith or dedication, or too much interested in money.

Mass transport, from the 1820s onward with the coming of the steam train, changed the face of tourism from an elite to a common enterprise for all classes and walks of life, but some aspects of early tourism remained difficult to discard. One is the elite commentaries and critiques, on which I will return to, the other is the almost categorical imperative to travel, within North Atlantic societies. Limited to the happy few earlier in history, the imperative is felt, at this stage, by an array of different people. In the present, not traveling is hardly conceivable: who has been nowhere, who has not a travel story to tell? To borrow a term used for the study of backpackers: one has to have 'road status' if one has any status at all. After each summer the first conversation turns to the holiday, with as a characteristic first question: 'Where have you been?' 'Home' is not an easy answer to give; at least it calls for excuses and clarification, with about the only respectable excuse being: 'We just moved and had to furbish our new home' (a new baby also helps!).

The elitist commentaries have also remained. The literature on tourism is replete with learned critiques of tourism, targeting especially mass tourism with scathing scorn, lashing out against the 'golden hordes' (Turner and Ash 1976) which have spoiled the old playgrounds of the rich and powerful. But, inevitably, the 'massification' of tourism, the 'routinization' of travel and the definition of a holiday as an almost inalienable right, are part and parcel of our post-modern society (Franklin 2003) and are here to stay.

After the train and, later, the car opened up Europe, cheap air travel in the last decade has put formerly remote continents within reach of large numbers of travelers from the '1st world'. Asia, the America's and Oceania all receive their share of tourists. Africa too, and it is the tourism towards and inside Africa that will occupy us here. Tourism is polymorphous, a many faceted jewel or a multi-headed monster—whatever metaphor one might prefer—and the interaction between tourists and receiving population, say 'hosts' and 'guests',[3] has many modalities. What interests us here are the effects and consequences of the new and strange situation that enables people from very different cultures to meet each other in the flesh, with both parties having to make sense of this strange occurrence. The main focus will not be on the tourist himself—enough has been written about him nowadays—but on the receiving population, the African 'hosts'. And these too, as will be seen, are varied enough. In order to glean the specificities of African tourism, we shall first look at the theoretical approaches in tourism studies, and then approach the characteristics of the African scene.

Theoretical approaches

As common and self evident as tourism has become, it has had to wait a relatively long period for scholarly attention: as an academic subject

---

[3] The terms 'host' and 'visitor' or 'guest' are used here, such as in Smith (1989), as a convenient short hand. In fact, the tourist encounter is quite dissimilar from the 'host'-'guest' relation, as Crick argues (1991: 328), the absence of balanced reciprocity being the most important difference.

it has only gained respectability during the last few decades (Jafari 2001). The anthropology of tourism as such started, one may say, with Valene Smith's edited volume *Host and Guests* (of 1974, 2nd ed. 1989), but the theoretical starter was the work of MacCannell on 'the theory of the leisure class' (MacCannell 1976), in fact a cultural critique of western civilisation. At least, MacCannell explained the phenomenon of tourism as a search for a lost authenticity: our western civilization has alienated its people from their cultural and existential roots, and holidaying was the means to make up for that deficit. Though in tune with the neo-Marxist tenor of the decade (i.e. the notion of alienation), this angle has remained important, even after the fall of the Berlin Wall, as it gave rise to a more anthropological and less evaluative angle (Butler and Hinch 1996, Lanfant 1995).

From the view of pilgrimage as tourism came the reverse: tourism as pilgrimage: 'if a pilgrim is half a tourist, a tourist is half a pilgrim' (Franklin 2003: 283). Victor Turner's work was seminal in this approach which sees holidays as a ritual, a time away from normal time, a liminal period in which the rules are suspended, even inverted (Graburn 1989, 2001). During these liminal times, like in rituals, the structures and distinctions of everyday life are not applicable; likewise, holiday time runs perpendicular to working time, and the tourist experience is in many ways the structural opposite of the usual living experience. John Urry (1985) took this lead farther and characterize the essence of tourism in the tourist gaze, the way a tourist looks and, by distancing, disengages himself from the object gazed at. A tourist looks, 'gazes', and, thus, separates himself from the observed—and lived-in—world. He does not participate in the world any longer as a normal, total person, but is reduced to a pair of eyes, and, most characteristically, a camera.

However, tourism itself is changing, a dynamic phenomenon if any. Increasingly, tourists are seeking bodily engagements, active leisure and material thrills. So, Franklin, in a critique of Urry, argues that in our post-modern society the notion of the 'tourist gaze' is less relevant than in the sight seeing decades of the mid to late twentieth century. Increasingly, tourists combine the senses, in packages which give a more complete existential experience, but which still differ fundamentally from daily life (Franklin 2003). In this, he shifts away from one fundamental element of this whole tourist-centred theoretical thinking, i.e. the notion of the fundamental strangeness of the tourist. The tourist phenomenon as an *explanandum* rests upon the scholarly surprise that people travel for amusement and spend a lot of money just in doing this.

Central to this debate is the major historical period of Romanticism. Most histories of tourism give ample space to the cultural influence of that era of European thinking (Nash 1996), and rightly so. Romanticism reshaped the perception of the environment, redefined 'nature' and reformulated some basic values of our civilization.

> The Romantic traveler was an exclusive figure: not only from the educated upper classes with the time and the resources to travel and ponder the world but also exclusive in the sense of excluding others. Essentially the Romantic traveler was a lone figure, needing to be alone in nature or in the silent appreciation of historical sites...(Franklin 2003: 35).

Child of an affluent Europe—and relevant only for the affluent minority in society—the Romantic view turned our attention away from ourselves—and from the church—towards our environment; as the wilds around us had been transformed and tamed, the forests of Europe changed from wild and dangerous places full of wolves, into well kept gardens. Nature became sought after, no longer feared. This domesticated nature was then liberated for esthetical considerations: nature was no longer to be conquered, mastered and tamed but to be admired, protected and cherished. As a critique of the conditions of early industrialism, the futility of human endeavour, Romanticism deplored the fleetingness of human existence and our distance from the surroundings. It is this view of nature, as something beyond us, something fragile and wonderful that still dominates within tourism, and in African tourism in particular, and is one of the dominant paradigms in the explanation of the phenomenon of *the tourist.*

The other angle focuses on the other end of the equation. History is full of irony. Romanticism coincided also with the start of the colonial expansion of Europe, thus with the subsequent 'rape of Africa'. The other major angle in tourism studies is the attention paid to the receiving population. Of course, tourism really took off after decolonization, but the similarities between the colonial project and tourism did not escape attention. From the dependencia approach came the notion that post-colonial developments tended to recreate colonial dependencies into complex but unequal relations between metropolis and satellite. In this light, the tourist experience in the third world—the one we are exploring here—was recognizably 'neo-colonial': the rich countries in the north descend on the poor South to wander in their pristine territories. Africa is one of those destinations where the 'West' goes to find adventure in the splendour of the game parks: the vast herds of wild beast thundering through the immense plains of untouched wilderness, the elusive 'big five' every traveler must have spotted and photographed. But Africa is also the continent of colorful, strange cultures, picturesque people, thatched huts in savannah surroundings, where one can encounter a truly 'other' culture. However, the airlines are from the North, the hotel chains are Western, the food is geared to Western tastes, the hotels are staffed with Europeans at the higher echelons, and most of the earnings go to the North anyway, the so-called 'leakage'. In short, Africa seems to become re-colonized by the North, this time not as a satellite state, but as a setting for exotic holidays. In this view the judgement on tourism is severe, even if a number of footnotes could be set at the equation tourism = neo-colonialism.

Anyway, one advantage of this approach is the attention given to the question of the impact of tourism on the Africans themselves. The majority of theoretical studies concentrate on the traveler, the 'guest' in the 'host and guest' equation, but the anthropology of tourism has taken the perspective of the host in the tourist encounter as its dominant angle, for two reasons (Chalmers 1997: 4–5). Firstly, the hosts are usually, in the case of third world tourism at least, the poorer population, the one being visited without the means for reciprocation of the visit, a type of population the anthropologists have been identifying with for a long time. The tourists, on the other hand, were of the rich *Homo sapiens* species, not prime research material for those who are used to studying 'down', not 'up'. Yet, for a proper understanding of tourism a paradigm is needed where the two are matched and combined. A theoretical approach of the 'host' side of the tourist equation can be embedded in a more general theory of cultural change, globalization/localization and internal cultural dynamics. This perspective is underdeveloped in literature.

The development of anthropological approaches is especially interesting when viewed by the various editions of the most seminal of all collections on anthropological studies of tourism, i.e. 'Host and Guests'. In the first edition (1974), the large majority of authors were extremely negative in relation to tourism, viewing it as a major disruption of local cultures, a dismaying commoditization of culture, if not an outright form of cultural prostitution. The 1989 edition witnessed a partial reversal of attitude: when updating their original pieces many authors changed their tune, spoke about some positive effects (income!) and noticed the flexible arrangements by local actors to accommodate both tourist, their own culture and their own privacy. Greenwood's piece on the Alarde festival in the Spanish Basque country is a good example. Still titled *Culture by the pound*—a negative title if any!—the first version was damning about the cultural impact of tourism:

> …it has become obvious that the increasing misdistribution of wealth and resultant social stratification are widespread results of tourist developments (Greenwood 1989: 179).

Somewhat later he invoked 'cultural commoditization and the loss of local autonomy in terms of 'final perversity' (ibid.: 180). In 1987 he noticed that the festival itself had become the arena for an internal political struggle, as well as a major tourist attraction, and noted the solutions the Basques had found to preserve both theatres, the political and the tourist one. So he asked:

> Are we correct that all local cultures are being destroyed? Or are they changing once again, under the press of circumstance and from their own dynamics, while we, as anthropologists, disapprove of the changes or at the very least do not comprehend them? (ibid.: 180).

He then positions his own change of heart within the changing theoretical debates within the profession, from 'traditional cultures' to the construction of identity, and from 'authenticity' to 'webs of significance' (ibid.: 183).

In 2001 Valene Smith, together with Maryann Brent published *Hosts and Guests revisited*, with a new set of cases. Though definitely about culture, the first mention of the impact of tourism is economic. For most of the articles the watershed has been crossed: tourism is simply there, important and interesting, beyond moral judgment. The quest for authenticity (Cohen 1988) has been abandoned in favour of sustainability, the notion of the preservation of cultures in favour of space for self determination and local agency, while finally the 'irridex' (the measure of irritation by tourists, Mowforth and Munt 1998: 249) gave way to the idea of 'separate realities' (van Beek 2003). In 1987 Smith discusses the question as to whether tourism was a major element in cultural change; in 2001 the general consensus, as she suggested earlier, was that tourism is a part of a bundle of major influences, and a minor player compared to the general trends of globalization and general cultural change (Smith and Brent 2001, Burns 1999).

However, this rightful retreat of judgment and this more widespread acceptance of tourism as a sub-phenomenon of globalization have left the theoretical field of the anthropology of tourism still open for development. Tourism does differ from most other aspects of globalization, and the communities that receive tourists do change, to some extent at least. Even if not the dominant player, some specific theory could account for the particularities of tourism in local communities. One major challenge is to study exactly the modalities of interchange between hosts and guests. The two sides, 'host' and 'guest', still leaves a third party unaccounted for, the intermediary organizations between them, the 'bubble'. The simple model 'traveler meets foreign culture' is inadequate. A sensitive travel writer told at a symposium of her train trip to Riga, Latvia:

> The whole trip and my whole stay in Riga I walked between two rows of people who were facing me, eager to accommodate my every wish, trying to make me comfortable. At one moment I realized that I could not see Riga because of them: they stood between me and Riga, between me and the Latvians, even if they were Latvians themselves. They made my stay possible while preventing me from really being there.

This is what was first called the 'environmental bubble' (Crick 1989) and is now called the 'tourist bubble'. It consists of those infrastructural arrangements that permit the professional reception of guests—such as hotels, lodges, personnel, logistics—plus those arrangements making the travel of tourists possible: travel agencies in the sending as well as in the host countries, transport facilities and a massive internet information business. This 'bubble' is where the tourist travels, arrives and is housed; this bubble protects the visitor from the unfortunate aspects of the destination while permitting some view to the outside. It is this bubble that interacts with the guest society, and so this bubble stands central to the dynamics of the tourist encounter. For the analysis of African tourism a closer look of this bubble will be important. In Africa the bubble consists of two parts, the one in the sending country described above, and the one in the African country, including local arrangements for travel and stay, local travel agencies, guides, game wardens etc. Evidently, there are many kinds of tourist arrangements, and some bubbles have thin, permeable walls, where people may pass through (such as a lodge for backpackers or local family guest accommodation), while others really enclose their guests. The clearest example of the latter are: cruise ships or isolated resorts, such as Club Med.

In the following, this notion of the bubble will be given more span and theoretical content, and will form the main focus for the study of tourism in Africa, as specifying the characteristics and dynamics of the various kinds of tourist bubbles seem to be crucial if we are to understand the varied impact of tourism upon African lives, and, thus, will be one of the challenges for African tourist research.

African tourism: paradoxes and contradictions

Africa is not the centre of world tourism, and will not be so for the foreseeable future, but tourism is important for Africa nevertheless. In order to appraise the importance for and the impact on Africa of tourism, the place of Africa in world tourism is crucial. A tourist is defined by the World Tourist Organisation as: someone who travels to another place or country and stays at least one night. For the statistics, to be presented below, this is of importance. Africa receives 3.6% of international tourist arrivals (Page 2005: 181), a figure that has been stable for the last decade. Viewing its land surface and population this is a clear under representation. The great tourism magnet is still the Mediterranean area, where over 40% of all world tourism is destined for, but also tourism to Asia amounts to 15% of arrivals and 19% in earnings (Dieke 2000: 16). The prognostics of the World Tourism Organisation foresees a doubling of tourism arrivals and revenues in the next 15 years, a growth of over 5% per year (WTO 1988, 1999) but it is doubtful whether the market share of Africa will increase significantly. Yet, for Africa it is important, and tourism investments are considered the most profitable in Africa (Sindiga 1999).

Not only is tourism unevenly distributed among continents, also within Africa the distribution of tourists between sub-regions and countries is extremely skewed; roughly speaking, in an Africa that includes the Maghrib, Northern Africa takes 33% of the market share, Southern Africa 31%, Eastern Africa 25%, Western Africa 10%, and the whole of Central Africa has to do with the remaining 1% (Dieke 2000: 18). Why this is so, and what the consequences of these large-scale figures for local populations are, can only be seen when we look at the specific characteristics of African tourism. So, in order to develop general insights about the interchanges between 'hosts' and 'guests', we have to view the specific character of specifically African tourism. These characteristics are viewed in the form of paradoxes and contradictions (van Beek 2003).

The spoiling tourist

The first paradox is mentioned in our introduction: from the start tourism has been an emotional, judgment-loaded subject. When the masses started to 'overrun' the pleasure spots of the happy few, the elite, in this case *academia*, retorted with severe condemnation: never would the sacred places of civilization be the same. And, to a large extent, this still is the case. 'Negative' or 'adverse' effects of tourism were routinely adduced, and tourism was easily evaluated as detrimental to local culture or regional ecologies. In the European context—the dominant one in international tourism—the beaches of the Mediterranean, the museums of the great cities and the few unspoilt places of the old continent would be trampled by the 'Golden Hordes' (Turner and Ash 1976). It seems the world was still good at the time of the Grand Tour, when the English gentleman, who had never had to earn a farthing, visited the cultural shrines of Southern Europe, experiencing his own renaissance as a cultural connoisseur. But mass tourism has been depicted as a moral catastrophe, a scourge on the land, disrupting local mores, commoditizing local cultures.

Tourism towards Africa developed as a full and legitimate child of European Romanticism. Africa has itself become an icon in European thought. More than any other 'foreign' continent Africa has become the epitome of the wilderness, of the untamed, of 'nature unspoilt', of pristine peoples. Against this background the judgmental character of tourist studies in Africa has assumed its own particular tone. Holiday making on the beaches of Europe... well one has a hard time considering that a serious subject, but eventually it could be studied with detachment from a neutral perspective. However, the rich Northerners regaling themselves on the wilds of Africa, gazing at the indigenous straw huts in order to go home with pictures of fierce lions, bare breasted 'ebony' women plus the views from their safari lodge, roused the ire of the profession. Both the spectacle of rich people gazing on poor Africans, and the inevitable show of wealth generated intense value judgments on the 'negative effects' of tourism. This evaluative aspect is not just in the African context important as tourism everywhere still generates evaluative comments, it is an elitist vision of cultural pessimism that still seems to dominate tourism and in which the African scene fits in well. The general feeling, among anthropologists as well, is that the unspoilt wilds and the untouched cultures are there for the scholar to study, and to report upon. Back home the people should be content just to buy their books and attend their magical lantern (now power point!) lectures. Tourists have no business trampling the African sites and tourism represents an environmental danger and a pernicious cultural and moral degradation.

For instance, in tourism to the Dogon area in Mali, till a decade ago, tourists were convinced the Dogon culture would be changing rapidly because of the tourist (i.e. their own!) presence. Most of the tourists had the 'explorer syndrome', trying to imagine that they were the first. Even if difficult to maintain, they could count themselves 'among the first' to visit the pristine area. Lately, the tenor has subtly changed. Now tourists are well aware of the intensity of Dogon tourism and its long history, and quite a few express the opinion that they must have been not the first but the last to see and witness Dogon culture in its pristine beauty.

Thus, the elitist view on African tourism is still very much en vogue, as it is in the case of most Third World locations. Of course, the main tourist spots in Africa are game parks, where the separation between sight and seer is artificially guaranteed, with full agreement of the tourist. But the idea that the tourist is a stranger who puts the very existence of the sight in jeopardy is very strong. Value judgments abound in tourist research in Africa as well; for other types of destinations, such as the beaches of Gambia or Mombasa, the 'loose morals' of tourism are easily invoked as a corrupting influence on local African culture.

Fearing Africa

A tourist brochure described an African holiday as a 'comfortable adventure', a wonderful phrase embodying the paradoxal nature of traveling in 'the wilds'. One main element is fear: tourists are scared of Africa. Africa is daunting, full of dangers, wild animals, people and illness. The foreign, exotic continent lacks security, hosts dangerous diseases and has a threatening strangeness: a 'wilderness'. Though that is part of its attraction, it does generate apprehension. This African tourism advertizing as a 'comfortable adventure', neatly encapsulates both the vision of the 'African wilds' and the wish to keep the wilderness at arm's length. A field observation from Mali:

> At the heart of the tourist season, just before Christmas, a bus with Dutch tourists arrived at a hotel in Mopti, Mali. The bus was a double one; its first part was standard, just filled with seats. Its second part

was closed and consisted of a series of small sleeping cubicles, one for each passenger. Of course, the bus carried enough clean water, food and cooking fuel to be totally self-sufficient. As such, that bus was a haven as well as a fortress: it hosted the westerners, at the same time shielding them from what they wanted to experience: Africa. In an area with very agreeable nights, where a simple cot with a mosquito net—in many instances even without one—would suffice, they relied on a totally structured westernised environment to be 'comfortable', thus foregoing the experience of the wide starry skies, or sleeping in the moonlight. And even with that equipment of an inclusive and movable 'bubble', they stayed in a hotel (van Beek 2003).

Others have commented on the element of fear as well; the apprehension is a constant companion of the traveler, but in Africa the motive becomes a dominant theme. It may be one reason why 'Africa' is for the tourist branch one destination. 'Africa is a country' a tour operator remarked, 'people choose between going to France, Mexico or Africa'. Not Kenya, South Africa or Mali, but a priori 'Africa'. Later, through the tour operator, a particular country is chosen. That is one reason that after the end of apartheid, South Africa has quickly gained dominance on the tourist scene, elbowing Kenya and Tanzania out of their former lead positions, while Zimbabwe, through its political unrest, has put itself out of the race. South Africa is seen as a white man's Africa, which generates confidence. African guides, also local ones, see this problem of 'fear' or apprehension quite clearly, often interpreting it as a question of trust. In Rhumsiki, the centre of the tourism to the Mandara Mountains of North Cameroon (van Beek 2003), the guides are acutely aware of the notion of 'trust' (*confiance*), as the basis of the tourist encounter. Characteristic is their low evaluation of fellow Cameroonians; stereotypes by Africans on Africans abound: 'The African will sell goat meat as steak', and 'the African tries to make an immediate gain, not thinking of tomorrow; for an African dishonesty pays, not honesty', and 'when the main hotel had a white *gérant*, the whites had confidence in hygiene, in price setting and in safety'. They themselves feel much more at ease with a European running the hotel, than with a Cameroonian at the helm (especially someone from the South of the country). Also, the former white *gérants* have stimulated and helped the school of Rhumsiki, also as a means of ridding themselves of most would-be guides. In itself, the lack of trust towards fellow nationals versus the (inflated) trust towards Europeans is a well-known phenomenon in Africa.

'Being there'

The third paradox is inherent in all tourism, but accrues with the distance in culture and the lack of familiar surroundings, i.e. the very concept of the tourist bubble. It is the notion of being in Africa, without really entering the African life. The tourist in Africa remains in game lodges, hotels, *campements*, bed & breakfast and has a very hard time participating in everyday African life, or in its highlights. This, of course, holds for all tourist experiences and destinations, and is the main theoretical characteristic of tourism as such: being there without 'being part'. But the bubble of travel arrangements, hotels, guest houses and lodges is more or less permeable: one can, by exerting oneself, go through the bubble wall. Some bubbles have thin walls, such as backpacker lodges, or at least have the ideology of having permeable walls (van Egmond 2005).

The 'environmental bubble' (Crick 1989: 327), or tourist bubble as it is now called, consists of the means created by both mediators and hosts to cushion the shock of the encounter, in this case to help the tourist encounter 'Africa' without fully experiencing it. MacCannell calls this the 'empty meeting place' (MacCannell 1992, 2001). This bubble also involves 'surrender'. The tourists surrender control over their daily decisions, and especially their mobility—the very thing that makes them tourists—to the tour operator, the travel agency, or the tour guide. During their journey they are continually told what to do, when to do it, and when to stop doing it:

> Surrender makes the details of travel so much easier, but in the bargain, the tourists also surrender their control of their relationship with the…people (Bruner & Kirschenblatt-Gimblett 1994: 237).

Usually the 'bubble' is the creation of the middlemen, who set up an itinerary and infrastructure guaranteeing comfort and some distance from reality. But also the host culture sets the stage for tourists, to show their life as they want to portray it, and as they perceive the tourists want to see it: a local culture tailor-made for visitors. Other authors speak about the 'tourist culture' (Bruner & Kirschenblatt-Gimblett 1994, Butler and Hinch 1996, Smith 1989) or the tourist as a 'natural victim'—of his own definition of reality (Crick 1989: 327). The 'bubble' not only produces comfort in the wilderness, it also filters and produces information about the other party in the encounter: on what is 'interesting' and 'authentic', on best places, spots, sights and activities. It provides a total and uncontested image of the other, both for the guests and for the hosts.

Africa as a parallel universe

In most tourist sites the surroundings are different, but the population is more or less familiar; familiar enough, at any rate, to consider them 'quaint and cute customs', stuff for the brochures and folkloric performances. In Africa the surroundings are different, sure, but not very diverse. African scenery does not change quickly; in fact, one can travel for long periods without seeing anything different at all. Part of the fascination of Africa, for people from the well-filled European countries, are those stretches of emptiness, the notion of space and the timelessness of traveling through vast stretches of identical surroundings. It is this notion of vastness, together with the fundamental strangeness of the inhabitants; first of all the animals, those that are not native to Europe and America, and, thus, emblematic for the African wilds. The big five form the main attraction because they are fundamentally alien: large, wild, undomesticated and in a world totally of their own. They are the animals that are, in a certain sense, on a par with human beings: they live in a world where humans do not belong, would be in danger and are of no importance anyway. Of course, a meerkat burrow is just as wild and alien, but too reminiscent of a human family, and they are afraid of humans, not the reverse. Animals, within the tourist focus, symbolize our awe and fear of the African wilderness. Our fascination is with a totally alien society, a parallel universe.

The African cultures which do command the tourist attention have the same element of strangeness. Maasai, for instance, are described as people that belong in the parks, not outside of them (Bruner and Kirschenblatt-Gimblett 1994, Corbey 1989), and generally the cultures of Africa are interesting as long as they are 'authentic', which means 'different' 'not European', in more than one sense 'wild'. This has two consequences.

First, tourists cherish their bubble more than in other destinations. Tourist brochures on Africa have three kinds of pictures: the majority is of wildlife, then a few shots of a nice sleeping arrangement—if possible with a half drawn mosquito net, a view of the outside and a picture of a terrace alongside a swimming pool—and, finally, one or two photos of smiling, authentic Africans. The largest pictures are always of a cheetah, lion or elephant. The tourist has to be comforted, put at ease: Africa can be trusted, or, at least, the bubble can be trusted. Important is what I like to call 'bubble authenticity': in Africa the bubble should be African. The hotel lodges are thatched, the woodwork has an African flavour, the mosquito nets have to be well in sight, both as an emblem of *Africanité*, and as a reassurance that the well being of the tourist is the first priority. And, the sleeping and eating arrangements have to be very near the main attractions, the animals. So, the view from the veranda is essential. For the more adventurous the bubble is represented by a picture of the 4 × 4 drive and a comforting photo of a sturdy tent.

Secondly, tourists are continually constructing Africa and looking for the 'real Africa'. In an Africa, which is only one destination, the tourist is looking for the 'essence' of the continent and constructs it as wildness, non-human and pristine. Africa is the continent before the coming of man, or before the coming of 'civilization'. For some, it is the continent of their roots, but for most it is the 'ultimate other', a parallel universe in the heart of our planet. This image of the essential Africa is easy to construct as well. The media show Africa in essentially two ways. The first, through the news channels and documentaries, is as a continent of suffering and crisis, with hunger and war reducing people to recipients of much needed charity donations. Africa has to be helped; at least, the people in Africa have to be kept alive by the rich North. The second way is through the adventure channels such as National Geographic, Animal Planet and Discovery; there, Africa is beasts, animals and people giving their best efforts to preserve the precious wildlife resources. These animal riches are considered as a part of the world heritage, not property or responsibility of the Africans themselves. Usually, it is white people interacting with the African game, not blacks (though they may help as game wardens) and few documentaries do not feature white people whispering titbits of interesting information on the animals into the camera. Here, as well, the message is clear: Africa is wild and has to remain that way, through our concerted (Northern) intervention.

Thus, the Romantic illusion is dominant in the image of Africa. Africa means time travel, to the era of our 'not-yet-existence'; African wildlife safaris are the present day alternative for the Grand Tour. The gentleman from Britain, gazing upon the ruins of the Parthenon in order to ponder upon the foundations of European civilization, finds his present counterpart in the couple from Germany training their

long telephoto lens on a shy rhino, savouring the African parallel
universe. The Romantic lie, as René Girard calls the bucolic life in
rural arcadia of early Europe, continues in the pictures of authentic
African life in the villages bordering the game parks.

Tourism without national histories

Romanticism went hand in hand with nationalism, one of the main
historic trends of the nineteenth century; every nation needs symbols,
concretes signs and historic places. What history is, is defined by
national interest: 'History is present politics', so symbols were revived,
created or adapted, thus, leading in Europe to a plethora of 'sights to
see' and an incipient 'massification' of tourism. In the Western world
early mass tourism revered, selected and often generated objects of
national inheritance, of overriding historical importance, suggesting
and symbolizing a unity which sometimes was spurious to start with.

> Despite the fact that nations are messy affairs with strange, unequal,
> contested and often violent biographies attaching to their mixtures of
> people, national tourist shrines often deliberately seek to assimilate
> all citizens in some way, to underlie the fact of their relevance and
> connection, no matter how shameful, scandalous or heroic their place
> in the national biographies may be (Franklin 2003: 130).

Most of these tourist shrines would be the buildings associated with
a dominant event in history; the famous open bus tour in London is
replete with history, but would, in fact, be quite uneventful without
the tales of kings and prelates, murderers and henchmen. The Bastille
in Paris has seen a web of mythology woven around it (during the
famous storming it seems to have been practically empty!) before
becoming the central symbol of the revolution. Some buildings have
acquired such tourist and symbolic importance almost by accident,
by just failing to be demolished; the Eiffel tower is an example. A few
combine supreme beauty with a telling, touching story, and become
almost universal human pilgrimage shrines: the Taj Mahal (Edensor
1998). Others are the genuine seats of history—the London Tower,
the Berlin Reichstag, the Anne Frank House in Amsterdam (Hartman
2001)—and in some the history is so supremely important that even if
the location itself is debatable it still attracts the tourist masses; Jesus'
burial tomb in Jerusalem is the clearest example, I think. Sometimes
objects are of crucial importance—Philadelphia's Liberty Bell, the British crown Jewels—sometimes graves or birth houses, like Napoleon's

grave. National governments have stimulated and financed this kind of tourism, first internally then internationally, as one of the best ways to stimulate a national unity. With a rising sense of ethnic consciousness, increasingly museums and monuments are produced for embattled minorities within countries. Recently, The Hague saw the unveiling of a memorial for the slave trade and slavery in Surinam. Typically, extremely relevant for the large minority of Surinamese extraction in the Netherlands, this monument generated a heated debate: who should do the unveiling, who should be present and who was it really meant for. Symbols of unity can also divide a country!

This pincer movement of nationalism, the rise of internal tourism and the creation of national stories of pride and victory has characterized the nineteenth and early twentieth century for North Atlantic countries, but has not happened in Africa, as yet. African nationalism is much more recent and still highly problematic, and—with the partial exception of South Africa—has created few national icons and no national tourism. Most African countries have not yet invented their relevant past and permanent signs of national unity and historic pride are almost absent.

However, in some countries people started to take up this challenge. Tourists visiting Dakar routinely go to Gorée, as one of the UNESCO recognized World Cultural Heritage Sites. High point of the Gorée tour is the visit to the *maison des esclaves*, and this serves as a splendid backdrop to the blood curdling tales about the export of slaves, the *voyage sans retour*. The actual historical fact that the smallish house did not serve as a housing for the merchants (upper floor) and the slaves (cellar) as the main trade was elsewhere and such an arrangement would not have suited the slavers at all, is of little import and does not deter from the grand unifying story of the slave trade. Relevant is the invention of 'history on the spot'. Another relevant example is evident in Mali. The building of national history needs national historic symbols. Mali has used the figure of Sunyata Keita for that purpose, the founder of the famous Mali empire in the—probably—thirteenth century. By a creative use of the oral traditions of their *jeli* (bard) class, Sunyata has become more of less the icon of the nation. Still, the historical realm of Sunyata was much larger, and it is debatable whether e.g. Guinée Conakry could not do the same. However, it is a question of policy, and Mali is quite eager to create national symbolism. The former president Konaré filled up available public space, mostly the round points at the major crossings, with a plethora of monuments, all new, in order to beautify the city and to give an impetus to national identity formation.

But in a continent with few old buildings, a poorly known history and a fragmentary and precarious national unity a lot of 'invention of symbols' still has to be undertaken. Just as well, national and regional tourism in Africa is still severely underdeveloped. Romanticism has not been a past of the African continent itself, and the detached, sentimental evaluation of nature and history are alien to the African nations. Indeed, Romanticism from the North has shaped Africa itself, not the reverse. When Africans become tourists, they do not visit their own country; few Malians from Bamako travel to view the famous Mosque of Djenné, and all visitors to the Dogon country, the hotspot of tourism in Mali, are from overseas: Europe, America, Japan. Africans visit family abroad, visit the great cities of Europe and generally are little interested in the historical and cultural repertoire of other African nations. South Africa and, maybe, Kenya are exceptions, but to some extent only. Kenya is reported to have experienced some internal and regional tourism, but that too seems to have been dominated by family visits (Sindiga 1999). South Africa experiences a considerable amount of internal African tourism, but here the white and Indian sub-populations dominate the tourist scene. This absence of internal tourism is a severe handicap for the further development of African tourism. Catering only to international tourists, as diverse as these may be, precludes both a suitable and flexible infrastructure and a sense of 'normality of the tourist': the tourist remains the stranger, the alien, and crossing the bubble wall will remain difficult.

The separation of destinations

Skewed distributions are what characterize African tourism. One major feature of African tourism is that the attractions for tourists are very unevenly distributed over the continent: game parks, beaches, culture, landscapes, historic sites, they are all located far apart, often in different parts of the continent. This, of course, is true of tourism everywhere, but one specific feature of African attractions is the narrow base for tourism per country and the separation between major attractions. The large majority of tourists come to Africa for wildlife: parks, game farms, hunting, photography etc. Though local peoples often are included, they are more of a 'side show' (Heath 2001). Part of the African parallel universe, is the notion of the 'Big Outdoors'.

For many tourists, especially in the South and the North, Africa is the place to escape into the wilds and to battle against a fierce, often desert environment. The Paris-Dakar Rally is an example, of course. But generally, crossing the sands by 4 × 4 is popular, through the Sahara or the Namib desert.

The third destination is a typical extension of Northern tourism, the sunny seaside, but only a few specific spots in Africa offer themselves for beach tourism. One peculiar version of this is 'romance tourism' (van Egmond 2005) either for women or for men, at different places though, in a typical inversion kind of holiday.

Less important, but up and coming, is African culture and history. Africa is for many tourists also a culturally pristine and authentic continent, where different cultures can be met in a direct way. Though not so much the continent of 'High Culture' with impressive buildings and ruins and well-known historical events, Africa is the continent of local communities with *authentic* cultures. A few destinations, like the Dogon in Mali, are specifically ethnic oriented, i.e. to those ethnic cultures rendered famous for whatever reason, anthropology included.

A very African attraction is heritage and roots tourism. Increasingly, Afro-Americans are visiting Africa to find their roots in the old continent. This may include some so-called thanato tourism, gazing upon the black side of history. From the slave deportation island of Gorée to the prison at Robben Island where Mandela spent many years, to the film set where the TV series *Shaka Zulu* was shot, the history of Africans has left at least some markers.

One of the problems for tourism development in Africa is that these destinations tend to lie each in a different country: a country like Mali has cultural assets, but is poor in wildlife; Namibia; is strong in game and open spaces, but has few cultural resources. Again, only South Africa, and to some extent Kenya, has a wider tourist basis, but generally the thesis holds for most countries: the tourist destinations are few and far between, and consequently ask for a varied approach (Go 1989).

Challenges for African tourism research

Now, viewing the theories of tourism and the peculiarities of the African tourist scene, what would be the research priorities for African tourism? First, as this article has started, our own pre-suppositions in relation to tourism research have to be examined continually and such a post-modern a priori would sit well with tourism research. On the topic of tourism many Africanists have not yet run the course from value judgment to the academic detachment of methodical relativism, and have not yet evolved beyond the 'negative'—'positive' dimensions of thinking. Anthropologists tend to fit in with the evaluations of 'their people' vis-à-vis tourism; my own experience in North Cameroon (Kapsiki) and Mali (Dogon) has tainted my attitude towards tourism. When I wanted to do research among the Kapsiki some time ago, a French colleague warned me: 'Les Kapsiki sont trop pourris par le tourisme', and actually that tourism was the reason no French ethnographer had selected the Kapsiki as yet. For the people in Rhumsiki, the picturesque hot spot of Kapsiki and Mandara tourism, their attitude was ambivalent at best. People did make money out of it, but the influence on the little children and youngsters was severely deplored as the continuous and almost inevitable begging for 'cadeau', 'bic' or 'bonbon' was frowned upon; the youngsters made a quick buck as a tourist guide and tried to get an invitation to Europe, also an aspect the elders of the village disliked. I soon began to share this attitude as well, though I realized it was only in that particular village that there was a 'problem' at all. Elsewhere life continued in the regular fashion, and even in Rhumsiki most of the time tourism was not an issue at all. When I came out to Dogon country, my tourism experiences intensified. A well known and an extremely exotic ethnography, intensive tourism (for Africa) of long standing and a cultural interest of the tourists had created a different kind of reaction from the locals (van Beek 2003). When my own work intensified the stream of tourists to my own field location this began to worry me, but my informants quickly allayed my fears, praising me for 'at last having done something worthwhile, i.e. bring in clients'. Thus, the positive side of tourism, the money made through it (van Beek 2005) and the contact with the outside became dominant aspects. Between the two periods of fieldwork tourism studies had come up with similar results and developed the 'bubble' concept, which was immediately recognizable to me. In those cases where local people react against tourist visits, it is unavoidable that the anthropologists follow suit; an example is Abbink's negative assessment of tourist encounters with the Suri of Ethiopia: the Suri dislike being visited and photographed and sometimes react violently against tourists who do not pay up (Abbink 2000).

So, where do we stand? Do we have to take a stand? Why is the honoured custom of cultural relativism so hard to adopt in tourism studies? Of course, the researcher easily assumes the role of the partisan spokesman, when the group he identifies with is under pressure, or is being exploited; and exploitation can be clear in tourist projects, as is the severe imbalance in wealth and power of the parties involved. Yet, our own proclivity for a certain type of argument, our inherent critique of the rich and powerful, our sensitivities towards exploitative relations and unequal exchanges may well block our view of other aspects of the tourist reality.

The second direction would be a 'tourist-impact-through-the-bubble' approach. This, evidently, cannot just concentrate on Africa, but on the general problem of host-guest encounters. Let us call it a theory of bubble formation, for the moment. Under what conditions and through what dynamics are tourist bubbles created, what are their respective characteristics and how 'governable' are they? This applies attention to the middlemen, both in tourist sending and receiving countries. Of all aspects of the tourist phenomenon the mediators have escaped by far the most attention. So, studies on the life trajectories of travel agencies, especially those dealing with African countries, would be very welcome. These 'bubble histories' would have to be approached using a comparative theoretical framework, where examples from Africa are matched with the large majority of studies, which come from outside the continent. The following reflections could serve as a model for such an approach.

The factors are, first of all, *environmental*: geographical isolation, the place within the tourist circuit, the place within the nation state, the volume of tourism and the provenance of the tourists (internal or international), as well as safety, would all play a role. An isolated situation, politically marginal, with a rapidly increasing tourist flow would not be conducive to the formation of an adequate reception structure and would lead to conflicts. The Ethiopian Suri are an example of such a situation, as are the Toraja in Indonesia (Crystal 1989) or fishing villages in Western Norway (Puijk 2001). Being at the heart of a tourism region, with a tourist industry at the heart of the nation, as well as a long history of a gradual increase in tourism, is a practical guarantee of creative and diversified bubble formation.

Islands, such as Malta or Aruba, may serve here as examples. In Africa the game parks of East Africa are, generally, in this position, but they preclude, to a certain degree, the direct interaction between guests. Finally, tourism is vulnerable to violence of various kinds: from street attacks and stealing, terrorism to civil war. Johannesburg, Egypt and 9/11, as well as Zimbabwe, are examples of this. Though a tourist stream can regenerate itself at a reasonably fast pace from violence-induced setbacks, the general insecurity of a continent such as Africa (which, after all is considered one destination) is a major obstacle. Tourism is an industry of images and the image of Africa as the lost continent is not conducive to tourist attention, or to tourist invest-ments, even if they are considered the best option at the moment in many African countries.

Other factors are more specific: the main tourist motivation, the niche width of the tourist attractions and the seasonality of tourists. It has been generally observed that if the host himself is interesting for the tourist, the bubble will be versatile and diversified, but also profitable for the hosts. The Amish 'bubble' in the USA, where a com-munity of fifteen thousand is 'shielded' from millions of tourist visits per year by a well-developed bubble, is an example of this (Fagence 2001). If the host lives in or near an attractive landscape, the niche width will be smaller and the bubble will be restricted and separated from the community itself, with more leakage and less bolstering of cultural self confidence. The Kapsiki of Cameroon are a case in point here, as is much of the Inca trail, but the African communities living near game parks are the most dominant examples of these factors.

The third set of factors is internal within the local community: the size of the group, the organisation of the group, the position of the group in the national context, the cultural self confidence (mentioned above), the cultural niche of the major attractions and local ecology. Small groups, such as the Bushmen, will have a harder time building a reception bubble, especially one that induces profit to the group itself. In strong hierarchical structures, such as those surrounding the Inca trail, internal divisions and local imbalances of power will tend to reproduce themselves in tourist arrangements and limit both the bubble formation from below, and local profits. As for the niche factor, if the main attraction is religious, for instance, participation of foreigners could be a problem. However, how this factor develops, depends very much on the religion in question. In Balinese tourism the temple rituals and the temple performances form a major part of the attraction, but this is a religion where foreigners are easily welcomed. And, anyway, Balinese tourism has a wide niche and an extremely adaptable and diversified bubble. On the other hand, Toraja tourism depends on exclusive rituals at the heart of their religion and building a bubble is more difficult there (Crystal 1989). Local ecology is a fundamental problem, especially in water scarce situations or whenever local populations stand more or less in the way of the tourist attractions. African game parks have experienced a lot of problematic interaction between game parks and the local population and the, often strained, relationship between people and parks has generated a lot of research and debate. The problem is, of course, that of the conflicting use of one environment in ways which are mutually exclusive. Solutions, such as the involvement of local population in game parks, gains and trophy hunting (e.g. ACASA and CAMPFIRE), are well known and show some of the dynamics mentioned above: the reproduction of national, regional and local imbalances of power within this part of the tourist bubble.

Finally, as always, the contingencies of history are important in relation to this debate. Tourism is set in a volatile world, amidst rapid changes and is very exposed to external threats. For the local hosts the main factor for flexible bubble development seems to be history of the tourist stream to the locality. A gradually developing tourist interest, both in numbers and diversity of tourists, seems to lead to a more integrated, diversified and flexible bubble on the spot, as well as more variety within the 'sending half' of the bubble.

The third major research question is that concerning the effect of these bubbles on the host populations. For this paradigm, which stems from a comparison between various case studies of tourist-guest interactions,[4] I would like to provide some leading hypotheses to be tested within tourism research. The general one is the conclusion of my own comparison between Kapsiki and Dogon tourist encounters (van Beek 2003)

> Tourism, as a peculiar aspect of global interaction, stimulates and reinforces processes of change and identity formation already existent in the local communities.

---

[4] Teaching a course on the anthropology of tourism at Utrecht University for some years, has stimulated this approach.

This stems primarily from my observations of the different reactions of Dogon and Kapsiki. The Dogon, who are fascinated by some aspects of their own culture, see this fascination mirrored in the tourists; the Kapsiki, who have a much lower 'cultural self confidence', perceive tourism as bypassing them in favour of the landscape.

Important for me here is, effectively, the concept of 'cultural self confidence', meaning the way in which people define their own identity in terms of culture. For Dogon, their collective identity hinges, for a large part, upon what they conceive as 'tèm', custom, displaying with pride their way of life to interested outsiders. Kapsiki tend to see their own culture as 'ancestral' and a thing of the past, though the general derogatory term 'Kirdi' (heathen) seems to be making a 'U turn' and, increasingly, is put forward as a term of distinction, as 'Kirditude'. Internationally, the most obvious case of a large sense of cultural self confidence would be Bali, which, as McKean argues, did not become 'less Balian' through its massive tourism, but 'more Balian' (McKean 1989: 120), a process which he calls 'cultural involution', in fact, the other side of the coin of 'cultural self confidence'.

A corollary is that *tourism generates views of the other consistent with the view of the self.* In meeting the other, one sees oneself, either in shared aspects, or in the opposites. The tourist encounter is an exchange of images in a complicated triangle of relations, tourist—mediators—local hosts. The tourist is armed with images of how 'the other 'should look, from travel books and guides, with the photographic high ground of the National Geographic Magazine as the ultimate yardstick. At the other end, the tourist itself is perceived in various ways depending upon the processes of their own collective identity definition. Again, the Dogon bubble views the tourist as a welcome stranger, a fellow human, who is interested in the same things which the Dogon themselves are; of course, the tourist is richer, so sharing with his host is normal, and as the Dogon give value for the tourist money, the tourist is expected to give money for the Dogon value (van Beek 2005, van Beek, Lemineur and Walther 2007).

In conclusion, African tourism approaches and research paradigms are, as Nunez and Lett have suggested (1989), more an application of general theory regarding the tourist situation than a specific 'tourism theory', but the translation from general—say globalization—theory to the field of tourism still needs to be made. In any field, environmental and internal factors have to be set within a historical narrative. Here the very marginality of Africa might work in favour of comparison and theory formation: the separation of destinations offers the possibility for a controlled comparison of, e.g., the factor destination and tourist interest on bubble formation and consequently, local impact. Africa is home to varied and quite specific tourist destinations, and is presently on the threshold of tourist development. If I have focused on theory in this article, it is because 'there is nothing as practical as a good theory'; after all, African tourism, though definitely not the medicine for all economic ills (de Kadt 1976), does offer an opening towards economic development, capitalizing on the specific and quite spectacular assets of the continent.

References

Abbink, J. 2000. *Tourism and its discontents. Suri-tourist encounters in southern Ethiopia*, Social Anthropology 8 (1) 1–17.

Bruner, E.M. and B. Kirschenblatt-Gimblett 1994. *Maasai on the lawn: Tourist realism in East Africa*, Cultural Anthropology 9 (4) 435–470.

Burns, P. 1999. *Tourism and Anthropology*. Cambridge: Cambridge University Press.

Butler, R. and T. Hinch 1996. *Tourism and Indigenous Peoples*. London: International Thomson Business Press.

Chambers, E. (ed.) 1997. *Tourism and Culture. An Applied Perspective*. New York: State University of New York Press.

Cohen, E. 1988. *Authenticity and commoditization in tourism*, Annals of Tourism Research 15, 467–486.

Corbey, R. 1989. *Wildheid en beschaving: de Europese verbeelding van Afrika*. Baarn: Ambo.

Crick, M. 1989. *Representations of international tourism in the social sciences*, Annual Review of Anthropology 18, 307–344.

Crystal, E. 1989. *Tourism in Toraja (Sulawesi, Indonesia)*. In V.L. Smith (ed.) Hosts and guests. The anthropology of tourism. 2nd ed. Philadelphia PA: University of Pennsylvania Press, 139–169.

de Kadt, E. 1976. *Tourism. Passport for Development?* Oxford: Oxford University Press.

Dieke, P. 2000. *The Political Economy of Tourism in Africa*. Washington DC: P. Cognizant Communication Corporation.

Edensor, T. 1998. *Tourists at the Taj. Performance and meaning at a symbolic site*. London: Routledge.

Fagence, M. 2001. *Tourism as a protective barrier for old order Amish and Manneonite communities*. In V. Smith and M. Brent (eds.) Hosts and Guests revisited. Washington DC: P. Cognizant Communication Corporation, 201–234.

Franklin, A. 2003. *Tourism, an Introduction*. London: Sage.

Go, F.M. 1989. *Appropriate marketing for travel destinations in developing nations*. In T.V. Singh, L. Theuns and M. Go (eds.) Towards appropriate tourism: The case of developing countries. Frankfurt Main: Peter Lang, 159–180.

Graburn, N.H. 1989. *Tourism and leisure: a theoretical overview*. In V.L. Smith (ed.) Hosts and guests. The anthropology of tourism. 2nd ed. Philadelphia PA: University of Pennsylvania Press, 21–36.

—— 2001. *Secular ritual: a general theory of tourism*. In V. Smith and M. Brent (eds.) Hosts and Guests revisited. Washington DC: P. Cognizant Communication Corporation, 42–50.

Greenwood, D.J. 1989. *Culture by the pound: an anthropological perspective on tourism as cultural commoditization*. In V.L. Smith (ed.) Hosts and guests. The anthropology of tourism. 2nd ed. Philadelphia PA: University of Pennsylvania Press, 171–186.

Hartman, R. 2001. *Tourism the Anne Frank House*. In. V.L. Smith and M. Brent (eds.) Hosts and Guests revisited. Tourism Issues for the 21st century. New York: Cognizant Corporation, 270–271.

Heath, R. 2001. *Wilderness tourism in Zimbabwe*. In V.L. Smith and M. Brent (eds.) Hosts and Guests revisited. Washington DC: P. Cognizant Communication Corporation, 319–332.

Jafari, J. 2001. *The scientification of tourism*. In V.L. Smith and M. Brent (eds.) Hosts and Guests revisited. Washington DC: P. Cognizant Communication Corporation, 28–41.

Lanfant, M.-F. 1995. *International tourism, internationalization and the challenge to identity*. In M.-F. Lanfant, J.B. Allcock and E.M. Bruner (eds.) International tourism. Identity and change. London: Sage, 1–43.

MacCannell, D. 1976. *The Tourist. A New Theory of the Leisure Class*. London: MacMillan.

—— 1992. *Empty meeting grounds*. The tourist papers. London: Routledge.

—— 2001. *The commodification of culture*. In V. Smith and M. Brent (eds.) Hosts and Guests revisited. Washington DC: P. Cognizant Communication Corporation, 380–390.

McKean, Ph.M. 1989. *Towards a theoretical analysis of tourism: economic dualism and cultural involution in Bali*. In V.L. Smith (ed.) Hosts and Guests. The anthropology of tourism, 2nd ed. Philadelphia PA: University of Pennsylvania Press, 119–138.

Mowforth, M. and I. Munt 1998. *Tourism and sustainability: development and tourism in the Third World*. London: Routledge.

Nash, D. 1996. *Anthropology of tourism*. Oxford: Pergamon.

Nunez, T. and J. Lett 1989. *Touristic studies in anthropological perspective*. In V.L. Smith (ed.) Hosts and guests. The anthropology of tourism. 2nd ed. Philadelphia PA: University of Pennsylvania Press, 265–280.

Page, S.J. 2005. *Transport and tourism: global perspectives*. 2nd ed. Harlow: Pearson.

Puijk, R. 2001. *Tourism in the Fjords and Mountains of Western Norway*. In V.L. Smith and M. Brent (eds.) Hosts and Guests revisited. Tourism Issues for the 21st century. New York: Cognizant Corporation, 175–183.

Sindiga, I. 1999. *Tourism and African development. Change and challenge of tourism in Kenya*. Aldershot, Ashgate, ASC.

Smith, V.L. (ed.) 1989. *Hosts and guests. The anthropology of tourism*. 2nd ed. Philadelphia PA: University of Pennsylvania Press.

—— 2001. *Hostility and hospitality: war and tourism*. In V. Smith and M. Brent (eds.) Hosts and Guests revisited. Washington DC: P. Cognizant Communication Corporation, 367–379.

—— 2001. *The nature of tourism*. In V. Smith and M. Brent (eds.) Hosts and Guests revisited. Washington DC: P. Cognizant Communication Corporation, 53–68.

Smith, V. and M. Brent (eds.) 2001. *Hosts and Guests revisited*. Washington DC: P. Cognizant Communication Corporation.

Turner, A. and T. Ash 1976. *The golden hordes: the anthropology of tourism*. Philadelphia PA: University of Pennsylvania Press.

Urry, J. 1985. *The tourist gaze: Leisure and travel in contemporary societies*. London: Sage.

van Beek, W.E.A. 2003. *African tourist encounters: Effects of tourism on two West African societies*, Africa 73 (2) 251–289.

—— 2005. *Walking wallets? Tourists at the Dogon falaise.* In S. Wooten (ed.) Wari matters: ethnographic explorations of money in the Mande world. Münster: Lit-Verlag, 191–216.

——, P. Lemineur and O. Walther 2007. *Tourisme et patrimoine au Mali. Destruction des valeurs anciennes ou valorisation concertée?* Cahier d'Études Africaines in press.

van Egmond, T. 2005. *Understanding the tourist phenomenon. An analysis of 'West'-'South' tourism.* Wageningen University.

WTO 1988. *Monograph on travel and tourism in Africa.* Geneva: World Tourism Organisation.

WTO 1999. *Tourism market trends: Africa 1989-1999.* Geneva: World Tourism Organisation.

Oliver Bakewell is based at the Department of International Development at Oxford University, where he is a Research Officer at the International Migration Institute, part of the James Martin 21st Century School.

His current research interests include discourses of migration, labelling and bureaucratic categories; forced migration, repatriation and humanitarian aid; the relationships between migration and development; changing patterns of international migration within Africa. He has a PhD and MSc in development studies from the University of Bath (UK) and a BA in mathematics from the University of Cambridge.

His recent publications include 'Uncovering Local Perspectives on Humanitarian Assistance and its Outcomes', *Disasters* (24 (2), 2000: 103–116); 'Repatriation: Angolan Refugees or Migrating Villagers?' in P. Essed, G. Frerks and J. Shrivers (eds) *Refugees and the Transformation of Society: Agency, Policies, Ethics and Politics* (New York and Oxford: Berghahn Books, 2004) and 'Community Services In Refugee Aid Programmes: Leading the Way in the Empowerment of Refugees or a Sop to Humanitarian Consciences', in F. Crepeau, D. Nakache, M. Collyer, N.H. Goetz, A. Hansen, R. Modi, A. Nadig, S. Spoljar-Vrzina and L.H. M.v. Willigen (eds) *Forced Migration And Global Processes: a view from forced migration studies* (Lanham MD: Lexington Books, 2006).

Walter van Beek is an anthropologist at the African Studies Centre in Leiden and has recently been appointed Professor of Religious Anthropology at the University of Tilburg in the Netherlands. He has done extensive research on two West-African groups, the Kapsiki/Higi of north Cameroon and northeastern Nigeria, and the Dogon of central Mali. His main research themes are religion, ecology and, more recently, tourism (as both his study areas are on the tourist circuit in West Africa). He has published widely on both groups and undertaken comparative work on religion in Africa, as well as on religion in general. His recent publications include an illustrated monograph, with S. Hollyman, entitled *Dogon; Africa's People of the Cliffs* (H. Abrams, 2001) and 'The Escalation of Witchcraft Accusations' in Gerrie ter Haar (ed.),

Imagining Evil. Witchcraft Beliefs and Accusations in Contemporary Africa (Africa World Press, 2007). His current theme links local religions, such as those of the Kapsiki/Higi and the Dogon, to the wider dynamics of religion in the world, like fundamentalism.

Mirjam de Bruijn is an anthropologist at the African Studies Centre in Leiden. Her research has a clear interdisciplinary character and an important theme is how people live and shape society in high-risk environments in both rural and urban areas. She has done fieldwork in Chad, Mali and Cameroon, where her research has developed around different themes: mobility and translocality, social (in)security, processes of in- and exclusion, and human rights. She recently started research on the relationship between mobility, social hierarchies and communication technology. Her publications include *Pastoralists under Pressure* (Brill, 1999), *Mobile Africa* (Brill, 2001) and *Climate and Society in Southern and Central Mali* (ASC, 2005). She is head of the 'Connections and Transformations: Society and Technology in Africa and Beyond' research group at the African Studies Centre.

Patrick Chabal, who trained in political science at Harvard, Columbia and Cambridge universities, is Professor at the University of London (King's College London). He has taught and done research in a number of (West, East and Southern) African countries as well as in the USA, France, Italy, Switzerland, India, Portugal and the UK. He is the author of a large number of articles on the history, politics, and culture of African countries. He is currently a member of the School of Social Science, Institute for Advanced Study, Princeton.

His main book publications are: *Culture Troubles: politics and the interpretation of meaning* [with J.-P. Daloz] (Chicago: Chicago University Press, 2006); *A History of Postcolonial Lusophone Africa* [with others] (Indianapolis: Indiana University Press, 2002); *Africa Works: disorder as political instrument* [with J.-P. Daloz] (Indianapolis: Indiana University Press, 1999); *The Postcolonial Literature of Lusophone Africa* [with others] (Evanston: Northwestern University Press, 1996); *Power in Africa: an essay in political interpretation* (New York: St Martin's Press/Macmillan, 1992 and 1994); *Political Domination in Africa: reflections on the limits of power* [Editor] (Cambridge: Cambridge University Press, 1986) and *Amílcar Cabral: Revolutionary Leadership and People's War* (Cambridge: Cambridge University Press, 1983).

Scarlett Cornelissen (PhD, University of Glasgow) is a senior lecturer in Political Science at the University of Stellenbosch, South Africa. Her current research interests include international urban trends and their implications for development in Southern Africa; migration and urban development in Southern Africa; and South African foreign policy. Aside from a single authored book on global tourism (*The global tourism system: governance, development and lessons from South Africa* (Ashgate, 2005)), she has co-edited three books (a two-volume review of globalization will appear with Palgrave in 2007) and she has published on a wide variety of topics in journals such as *Review of International Political Economy, Journal of Modern African Studies* and *Third World Quarterly*.

Rijk van Dijk is an anthropologist at the African Studies Centre in Leiden. He has done extensive research on the rise of Pentecostal movements in urban areas of Malawi and Ghana and is the author of *Young Malawian Puritans* (ISOR Press, 1993). He co-edited *Modernity on a Shoestring* with Richard Fardon and Wim van Binsbergen (EIDOS, 1999), *The Quest for Fruition through Ngoma* with Ria Reis and Marja Spierenberg (James Currey, 2000) and *Situating Globality: African Agency in the Appropriation of Global Culture* with Wim van Binsbergen (Brill, 2004). His current research focuses on the transnational dimensions of Ghanaian Pentecostalism, in particular in relation to the migration of Ghanaians to the Netherlands and Botswana.

Ulf Engel, who trained in political science at Hamburg University, is Professor 'Politics in Africa' at the University of Leipzig. He has taught at Stellenbosch (South Africa) and Dalhousie (Halifax, Canada) universities and done research in a number of Anglophone African countries, including Zimbabwe, Malawi, Tanzania, South Africa, Nigeria and Ethiopia. He is Director of Studies of the master programme African Studies at Leipzig and spokesperson of the PhD Research Training Group 'Critical Junctures of Globalization'.

His main publications include: *The African Exception* (Aldershot: Ashgate, 2005, co-edited with G.R. Olsen), *Is Violence Inevitable in Africa?* (Leiden: Brill Publishers, co-edited with P. Chabal and A.M. Gentili), *Africa and the North* (London: Routledge, 2005, co-edited with G.R. Olsen), *Die Afrikapolitik der Bundesrepublik Deutschland 1949-1999* (Hamburg: Lit-Verlag, 2000), *Die beiden deutschen Staaten in Afrika* (Hamburg:

Institut für Afrika-Kunde, 1998, with H.-G. Schleicher), *The Foreign Policy of Zimbabwe* (Hamburg: Institut für Afrika-Kunde, 1994).

Bodil Folke Frederiksen is Associate Professor at the Institute of Society and Globalisation at Roskilde University, Denmark. She teaches International Development Studies. Her current research interests are: gender and generation in urban situations; popular culture and mass media in Africa; the construction of 'knowledge' of sexuality in colonial and post-colonial situations, lives and (auto)biography, political culture and public spheres in Africa.

Recent publications: "Writing, Self-Realization and Community: Henry Muoria and the Creation of a Nationalist Public Sphere in Kenya" in *Current Writing* (18 (4), 2006, 150–166) and "The Present Battle is the Brain Battle": Writing and Publishing a Kikuyu Newspaper in the Pre-Mau Mau Period in Kenya in Karin Barber (ed.) *Africa's Hidden Histories: Everyday Literacy and Making the Self* (Bloomington and Indianapolis: Indiana University Press, 2006: 278–318).

Jan-Bart Gewald is a social historian of Africa at the African Studies Centre in Leiden. His research has covered topics as diverse as the ramifications of genocide in Rwanda and Namibia and the socio-cultural parameters of trans-desert trade in Africa. He has also conducted research on pan-Africanism in Ghana, spirit possession in Niger, Dutch development cooperation, Africa in the context of globalization, and social history in Eritrea. He is currently researching the socio-economic implications of the motor car in Zambia, having been awarded funding by the Netherlands Organisation for Scientific Research (NWO) for a five-year inter-institutional multidisciplinary research programme entitled 'ICE in Africa: The Relationship between People and the Internal Combustion Engine in Africa'. His publications include *Herero Heroes: A Socio-political History of the Herero of Namibia 1890–1923* (James Curry/David Philips/Ohio University Press, 1999) and, with Jeremy Silvester, *Words Cannot Be Found: German Colonial Rule in Namibia, An Annotated Reprint of the 1918 Blue Book* (Brill, 2003).

Leo de Haan is geographer by training and published widely on African livelihoods. He directed research at universities of Amsterdam and Nijmegen and is currently director of the African Studies Centre Leiden and professor in African development.

His main publications are with A. Zoomers 'Exploring the Frontier of Livelihood Research' in *Development and Change* (36 (1), 2005: 27–47); 'The livelihood approach and African livelihoods' in: P. van Lindert, A. de Jong, G. Nijenhuis and G. van Westen, *Development Matters. Geographical studies on development processes and policies* (Utrecht: Utrecht University, pp. 139–156, 2006) and *Agriculteurs et Eleveurs au Nord-Bénin. Ecologie et genres de vie* (Paris: Editions Karthala, 1997).

Hein de Haas is a Research Officer at the International Migration Institute, part of the James Martin 21st Century School at the University of Oxford. His research focuses on the reciprocal linkages between migration and broader development processes, primarily from the perspective of migrant-sending societies. He did extensive fieldwork in the Middle East and North Africa and, particularly, Morocco. His current research interests include migration and development, migration transitions, trans-Saharan migration from West Africa to North Africa, and socio-spatial transformations of Saharan oases. He has a PhD in development studies (Radboud University of Nijmegen, the Netherlands) and an MA (*cum laude*) in human and environmental geography (University of Amsterdam). His main publications are *Irregular migration from West Africa to North Africa and the European Union* (Geneva: International Organisation for Migration, forthcoming); 'Morocco's migration experience: a transitional perspective', forthcoming in *Inter-national Migration*; 'International migration, remittances and development: myths and facts in *Third World Quarterly* (26 (8), 2005: 1269–1284); 'Migration, Remittances and Regional Development in Morocco' in *Geoforum* (37 (4), 2006: 565–580) and with Roald Plug 'Trends in migrant remittances from Europe to Morocco' 1970–2005 in *International Migration Review* (40 (3), 2006).

Carola Lentz is professor of social anthropology at the Department of Anthropology and African Studies, University of Mainz (Germany). She has been conducting research on labor migration, ethnicity, the history of chieftaincy and the politics of belonging in Northern Ghana since 1987. For the past years, her focus was on the history of mobility, land and property rights in Burkina Faso and Ghana. Current research explores changing career strategies and home ties of Northern Ghanaian elite men and women. Author of *Ethnicity and the*

Making of History in Northern Ghana (Edinburgh, 2006) and numerous journal articles, she has edited several volumes, including *Changing Food Habits* (London/New York/Amsterdam 1999); *Ethnicity in Ghana: The Limits of Invention* (London, 2000); *Histoire du peuplement et relations interethniques au Burkina Faso* (Paris, 2003) and *Land and the Politics of Belonging in West Africa* (Leiden, 2006).

Alain Ricard, directeur de recherche (CNRS-LLACAN), is a member of the Graduate school of the Institute for Oriental languages (INALCO) in Paris. He was head of the French institute for research in Africa (IFRA), in Nairobi (1989–1992): his book, *Languages and literatures of Africa*, was published in English (James Currey, 2004). In French he recently produced a short version of this history: *Histoire des littératures de l'Afrique subsaharienne* (Paris, Ellipse, 2006), as well as a collection of essays, *La Formule Bardey, voyages africains* (Bordeaux, Confluences, 2005).

INDEX

Page numbers followed by a t refer to tables.